ID0996823

ONE FLEW OVER THE CLUBHOUSE

Also by Tom O'Connor and published by Robson Books

From the Wood to the Tees
The World's Worst Jokes

ONE FLEW OVER THE CLUBHOUSE

Amusing Shots from his Golfing Bag

Tom O'Connor

Robson Books

First published in Great Britain in 1993 by
Robson Books Ltd,
Bolsover House, 5–6 Clipstone Street, London W1P 7EB

British Library Cataloguing in Publication data
A catalogue record for this title is available from the British Library

ISBN 0 86051 890 6

Illustrated by JIM HUTCHINGS

Photoset by Selwood Systems, Midsomer Norton
Printed and bound in Great Britain by
Butler & Tanner Ltd, Frome and London

To Bob!

For Keir.
One day we'll have that game.

Best wishes

'Your first book was responsible for the sale of thousands of golf clubs – I sold mine straight away.'
Unknown admirer

Contents

1

Why? What For?

TO BE honest I didn't fancy writing this book. I mean, the sum total of my golfing knowledge would hardly fill the sleeve of a Woodbine packet (now there's a sign of age and a misspent youth). So why try to follow up a relatively successful first golf book? Why not quit before I'm found out?

For the answer we must consult that stern barometer of public taste, my publisher. He phoned and said: 'Now look here, the first one was such a hit, you owe it to your public to try again.'

A bit tactless of him to call it a 'hit', as we shall see. Picture me, a few days after publication, on a coolish autumn morning making up a four-ball at Royal Ascot golf club. Strolling up to the ball after my first drive (not a bad one), I came face to face with the most dangerous phenomenon in golf – a player who cannot tell which hand is which – or, in the vernacular, doesn't know his Rs from his Ls. Slicing his tee shot off the 6th, he shouted down wind 'Fore left' when he meant 'Fore right'. I turned to see where his ball had gone and found myself leaning into a drive that was straight out of the screws.

I remember the blow, and I remember thinking 'What a silly chap' (or words to that effect). Then I keeled over, struck my head on one of the clubs in my bag, and passed out. (The technically minded will want to know that examination of the wound proved that I hit my head on my 7-iron.)

What a to-do! I'd like to report that I came to and manfully completed the round, but can't do so. Following a shot from my partner's hip flask – whisky and Drambuie mixed (honestly!) – I was 'escorted' back to the clubhouse for treatment and further medication.

The showbiz bush telegraph is the fastest in the world, and before I knew it the press was on to the story. At least one tabloid had me in glorious colour on a golf course alongside a banner headline that bellowed: 'Tom almost killed in golf accident.' This sparked off a raft of phone calls from family, friends and even people overseas whose relatives had passed on the story. Well, you know how these things develop, and before long I began to embroider the incident a little so as not to disappoint anyone.

'Did you take long to recover?'

'Well, quite a while.'

'Does it hurt still?'

'Only when I laugh.'

'Where did the ball hit you?'

'It missed my shoulder by eight inches – caught me smack on the forehead.'

So started a remarkable sequence of events. Publisher on phone: 'The press seem to believe that you nearly died on the course.'

Tom: 'Never! Died on my feet on stage, but hardly a headache from the golf ball.'

Pub: 'Well, all right, but at least it sounds interestingly serious, and we *do* have a book to sell.'

Tom: 'You mean they're more interested in my near demise than my literary prowess.'

Pub: 'But of course, old chap.'

Tom: 'OK. So what happens now?'

Pub: 'Let me tell you the plan....'

And so it began. A round not of golf but of radio and TV shows telling of my accident and displaying my shiner and slashed temple and occasionally getting in a quote from the book. Boy, did it arouse interest!

First up I was invited to BBC Pebble Mill's lunchtime programme to be interviewed by my old mate Judy Spiers, a great giggler with a lovely sense of humour – ideal for the show she hosts. My pals at the BBC had laid on a mass of props to set up my entrance: golf bag, clubs, plastic balls to hit into the audience and one or two other goodies I hadn't bargained for.

But my luckiest break was with the programme's running order. I was down to follow the Chippendales, who were there to sing their latest single. They were great – mucho macho and perfectly in synch – and while they were on I nipped down to Make-Up and had my head swathed in yards of bandage, like an American Civil War hero, on to which liberal dollops of fake blood were dabbed.

On my entrance I hit a ball into the audience, then staggered down to Judy and collapsed into a chair.

'My God, what happened to you?'

'Oh, I had a punch up with the Chippendales – but I soon sorted them out.'

So, the interview having got off to a good start, we had a long chat about the book. At last, before winding up, Judy asked me to have a look in the golf bag. Sure enough, there was a copy of my book, which I was able to flash onto the screen.

'Talking of flashing,' remarked Judy casually, 'what else is in the bag?' I reached in – and pulled out several handfuls of ladies' underwear, apparently collected from the stage after one of the Chippendales' concerts.

'This is all new to me,' I protested. 'I'm more used to a volley of pension books and thermal vests.' And as if someone had anticipated my reaction, a shower of these very items descended on me, making a perfect end to the interview. Thanks, Judy. Thanks, Pebble Mill.

In fact, I owe a debt to all the radio presenters on BBC, Capital and many regional stations who made time to talk to me. In particular I must put in a word for Radio Norfolk for a display of patience and forbearance beyond the call of duty. The station had wanted me to do a live face-to-face chat. Unfortunately, I could not fit the long journey to Norwich and back into what was then a very hectic cabaret schedule. So we settled for a live phone-in, the next best thing (it says here).

Owing to the programme schedule, it soon became apparent that I would be en route to a cabaret venue at the time of the phone-in. No problem: my wife Pat took the wheel, and I sat beside her, mobile phone in hand. What I hadn't realized was that members of my family had been calling the world from the car and the phone's battery was expiring. Bang on time, the phone rang, and I just had time to say hello to the radio presenter before the set died on me and I was off the air.

Desperate times call for desperate measures and it was Pat who came to the rescue. Pulling into a lay-by on the A3, she parked by its mobile caff and found another motorist with a mobile phone. She explained our problem, and he generously offered the use of his phone. I called up Radio Norfolk, got the programme's producer on the line, and asked him to call me back so as to save our Good Samaritan a few bob.

And so the phone-in went ahead, thanks to Jay, our fellow motorist. In fact, the story was so good that Jay spent almost as much time on air as I did, and me chipping in now and then with: 'Oh, by the way, I've got a new book out!'

Good day. Good interview. Good bloke, Jay.

I could fill a book with thanks to all the good people in the press, radio and TV who gave me time or space to talk about my book. But I must mention Gay Byrne and his *Late Late Show* in Ireland. 'The Man' has been my friend from way back, and although I had appeared on his show earlier in the year, he brought me back to air my golfing views and helped to popularize the book 'over the water'. So in deference to Gay, no Irish stories in this book. Oh well, maybe just the one I picked up at Portmarnock golf club.

A senior member comes off the 18th green and the pro says: 'How did it go today, Dermot?'

'Well,' says Dermot, 'I didn't play my usual game. But then, I never do!'

No more, I promise. (Well, maybe just a few later on.)

So anyway, a few weeks later I get a jubilant call from my publisher, who reports that the book is selling well in Britain and elsewhere. 'My sales people tell me the cut on the head did it. So next time ...'

'Don't tell me,' says I, 'Next time I lose a leg – right?'

'Good man! I knew you'd see it our way.'

If my cut head makes me want to do anything more in the golf world, it is to make a new rule. All golfers (whether they know which hand is which or not) should shout 'fore knife side' or 'fore fork side' – sounds daft but it might save a few accidents. Trouble is, golf is a game of the gods played by mere mortals, and unusually fallible ones at that. Even 'knife side' and 'fork side' may have different meanings for people who, like many Americans, eat with the fork in their right hand. And there's another potential problem. My older readers may remember the old National Service gag where the sergeant-major bellows: 'Company, left ... *turn!*', whereupon the young recruit calls out: 'Sergeant-major, is that your left or ours?'

Now at this very moment I can sense classier, low-handicap golfers getting impatient to point out that there is a very simple solution to the problem which is in general use among tournament pros: namely, to raise the appropriate arm sideways at the same time as shouting 'Fore!' Well, yes – it certainly is a simple and sensible solution. But, quite apart from the fact that I know plenty of hackers who, at least after the lunch interval, couldn't necessarily be relied upon to coordinate voice and arm movements, I frequently move in golfing circles where a simple and sensible solution to *any* problem is regarded with suspicion. It goes against that philosophical grain in their characters which attracted them to golf in the first place. These are deep waters, Watson.

Golfing accidents and incidents and lunacies is what this book is all about. Let me try to take you through a fairly average round. No, not the one where everything goes like clockwork – tee shot down the middle of the fairway; second shot onto the green; two putts.

Come on, when did you *ever* have a round like that? (OK, Seve, you can skip this bit!) No, I mean the average round that starts badly and fades away. Rough to deep rough and back again. Religious golf – across here, then across there. At times like these your ball has more smiles than a clown and one's mind is filled with reflections of a philosophical nature. Reflections like:

'What the hell am I doing here?'

'Call this relaxation?'

'I could have been wall-papering the bedroom.'

'The wife thinks I'm enjoying myself.'

I call to mind the plaintive cry of a member of the Ascot 'youth club' (over 70s) who'd just duffed his second shot: 'Forty years of playing and I'm still trying something new.'

But that's the point. We golf fanatics are convinced, despite all the indications to the contrary, that something new, some inspirational gimmick, will suddenly transform our whole game and turn us into tournament pros. We are forever in pursuit

15

'Still trying something new.'

of the loadstone, the holy grail. (Well, it's more fun than two hours a week on the practice ground, dammit.) One day my mate Paul ran into the club-house shouting, 'I've found the answer'. We started to call him 'the Quizmaster'. Of course, he lost the 'answer' just as quickly. So now we call him 'Daisy' (some days 'e plays well and other days 'e doesn't).

Paul, being a publican, plays with a very heavy team and it's always a challenge when they have a golf day. It generally consists of 18 or so players, hung over from yesterday, topping up at the first with 'heart starters', then pausing at every green for a 'freshener'. By the sixth the game is reduced to trying to remember who you are! I played with this lot last year and I'm still not sure of my identity.

'Why do we play golf?' is a question that's both deep and daft. Personally, I play because golf is a sport I can live with comfortably. In my youth I tried soccer. Not for me. I remember having a trial for Everton colts team and the local newspaper critic reporting: 'O'Connor is amazing – he can trap a ball further than most people can kick it.' In my teens I tried boxing. Not for me. I could just about live with the half hundredweight of gumshield in my gob; I could put up with the odour of armpits. But I drew the line at being thumped about. In fact, on the night of my first ever bout I was disqualified for using my head – I never turned up.

Then, in my 30s, I tried golf. I liked it – it's for me. A great sport played at the right time of day, at the right place, and with congenial companions. Without any facetious intent I can say that golf helps me to exercise three of life's great gifts:

'Faith' in almost any idea or advice or appliance

which promises to make the game easier. 'Hope' that I will improve my game; and 'Charity' through participating in Pro-Ams and other great fund-raising events.

Lord of the Links – we are all believers. Just show us the way!

2

Every Golfer is a Nicklaus – Just Under-equipped

LOOK – I'M not an envious person. I begrudge nobody their success or good fortune. Like most golfers I get more satisfaction from personal achievement than from outright victory. What I mean is, I'd rather play well and lose than play badly and win.

I do not envy the gifted – the Faldos, Woosnams, Crenshaws – but sometimes they make me wish ... well, you know, that I had a *little* of their talent. But as in golf, so in life – don't we always wish we had a little of others' abilities – say, for instance, the art of instant repartee.

Take the story of the bloke in a Porsche travelling along the motorway at about 75mph. A police car trailing him decides to glide behind him – just to make its presence known and make the Porsche drop 5mph. However, the driver, seeing the police in his mirror, accelerates to 85mph.

In response, the police switch on the flashing blue light – and the Porsche accelerates to 100mph. Now the police turn on the siren, but the Porsche goes up to 120mph.

Eventually, with the help of a strong tail-wind, the patrol car pulls alongside the Porsche and flags it down. With the customary hitch of the trousers, the two bobbies approach the driver: 'Evening, Ayrton. Care to explain why you saw the blue light and went faster, you heard the siren and went even faster, and didn't slow down till we drew alongside?'

'Well, it's like this officer,' says Mr Repartee, 'two weeks ago my wife ran away with a policeman, and I thought he was bringing her back!''

It's that kind of inspiration we need, so that one day, out of the blue, we might discover the perfect golf swing. (And pigs might fly.) In other words, at our level golf is all about finding a short cut to success.

Maybe it can be found in instructions from a pro:

'Keep your head down!'

'Keep the left arm straight!'

'Slow down your take-away!'

Or the most hurtful words ever said to me: 'If I were you, I'd have two more lessons and then pack up altogether!'

Seriously, though, sometimes we find that following the pro's advice is too much like hard work. We forget how many hours of practice it can take to perfect even one stroke. Ben Hogan, who hit more perfect shots than any golfer in history, practised for hours on end every day of the week. Jack Nicklaus in his prime reckoned he was lucky if he hit one more or less perfect shot in the course of a round.

Think of the free-kick setpiece in soccer. Don't tell me it just happens or that the ploy they adopt is the only option open to the players. No, they've probably three or four variations lined up, each one the result of many, many hours, even days, of rehearsal. Yet here we go, staggering into the rough and wondering whether to use a 3 or 5-wood to a ball that's almost invisibly entangled in what appears to be mangrove swamp.

Something has got to be done – but what? We're looking for the maximum return from the minimum of effort – so that means professional advice and lessons are the last resort. It's very odd that even many wealthy hackers reject the idea of paying for lessons from a qualified coach, which is the only way to (more or less) guarantee an improvement in one's game.

Practice takes too long – it's boring anyway, and we've more important things to do with our time. How about buying success? Now you and I know we'd pay almost anything to instantly improve our play, so herein lies the answer. You'd think that would be impossible but it's not – thanks to the gadget, the gizmo, the gimmick.

Yes, brothers and sisters, the gadget will be our redeemer – all hail to the (latest) greatest invention of the age! Come bathe in the glory of the plastic panacea – the cure for all our ills – the one pure light in a world of golfing darkness. We seekers after redemption on the fairways are a strange mixture of the cynical and the credulous. We may mistrust advertising hype, we may ignore the kindly advice of a passing member of the club who plays off scratch and happens to notice one of the grosser errors in our swing. No – the words we treat as the true gospel have a wonderful simplicity and conviction:

'My mate says it's foolproof!'

At last – the final answer, the ultimate revelation, the reason why we've never cracked the game before. Now we know because of somebody's mate. And the answer is a gadget. But hang on a minute. Which gadget? There's a veritable Aladdin's cave of 'foolproof' gadgets.

Well, let's start with the basics. Didn't the pro once tell you that it was important to keep the left arm straight? (It was the pro wasn't it? Well, if it wasn't him it was someone else who knew – maybe I read it in a book.) Anyway – it *is* important to keep your left arm straight, so let's concentrate on that. Can we find a gadget to deal with this problem? But of course we can!

Funnily enough, a man whose ingenuity I much admire made many thousands, if not millions, of pounds, dollars, yen and other coinage by advertising the secret apparatus to lower your handicap overnight (Send cash with your order). The miracle cure came in the form of a splint to strap onto the left elbow, thus preventing it from bending. Hence the left arm stays straight. So that's the answer. Or is it?

Well, despite the sale of millions of splints (and the manufacture of home-made copies, usually from rolled-up newspapers and some sticky tape), there doesn't seem to have been an overnight slashing of handicaps. Maybe there's just one more thing we need. Think back! The oracle said: 'Keep the left arm straight.' The wrist is part of the arm and of course the wrist bends. Hey, that's it! The wrist is breaking at the critical moment and that's causing a 'bend' of the straight left arm.

Heavens, why didn't we think of that before? It's

'Now, what about the other arm, dear, or is that all right?'

so obvious – what mugs we've been. Now, is there a gadget to stiffen the wrist? Of course there is! Basically, it's a small splint (the really pukka model is shaped a little like a shoe horn) which slips into the glove and prevents easy wrist movement. This *must* be the answer.

If this is all that has been needed to unlock the golfing key, why not make a lasting investment in your game? Instead of splints hither and yon, why not go the whole hog? Why not have the whole left arm encased in plaster? It will be much cheaper long term and will look less daft than an arm full of timber.

But what's this? The stiff left side doesn't provide constant steady improvement. All right, maybe one or two shots better than before but still not perfection. Maybe we need more practice with the gadgets – but hold up. We bought them so we wouldn't *have* to practise!

At this point, credulity having done its worst, another aspect of hacker psychology takes over. 'Just a minute,' says the brain, 'maybe all my pals are having success with their splints. Maybe it's only me who's failing. Yes, that's what it is – I'm the odd one out – sad Sam, Mr Unfortunate. The others are probably trying not to upset me talking about it when I'm with them. Boy, am I unlucky! If it was raining soup, I'd be standing here with a fork in my hand.'

In other words, rampant paranoia. What to do? Suicide? Impossible – the way you're putting, if you threw yourself under a bus you'd miss! Well, there's only one alternative: tell your friends about your problem. Go on, be brave, they won't laugh.

Strangely enough their reaction may amaze you. You may find that they too are having private nightmares. So you start comparing notes. The left-side theory isn't working. Why? – should there have been a magic word to say? Maybe there was something in the instruction manual we overlooked. (A prayer, maybe?)

Go back in time, go back to some of those other words of wisdom uttered by the pro, or written in one of the scores of 'basics of golf' books now rotting in the garden shed or vouchsafed by some bloke in the pub. Wasn't there something about swaying. Yes, that's it! Swaying – of course that's it, folks. How stupid we've all been – we forgot the golden rule of gadgetry: when the left side is encased in swathings it may try to perform its own robotic movement and will force the entire torso to *sway* instead of turning on its axis.

Forget the plaster cast. It's too drastic and causes too much swaying. Go back to basics – go back to the substance which rules over all – wood! Yes, wood will stop the sway. Wood and science – let's think about that for a while. (Do you know, I'm beginning to think that if I'd spent the amount of time practising that I've spent strapping myself up and worrying, I'd probably not need the gadgets. But no – that's traitor's talk. Back to the wood.)

Gather round friends and observe the 'wee wedge', the fruit of modern technology, superior intelligence and desperation. A foot long, half a foot wide, four inches high. A block of wood of perfect size, just as our latest prophet ordained. Now split it diagonally down the length and we have two answers in one: a foot-long wedge of wood to place under the right foot, making it rigid during the swing. If the right side is jammed by the block, the body won't sway, the left arm stays in the proper plane, and Bob's your uncle.

I could go on for days expounding theories about the mechanics of golf. They are unquestionably sound theories and have long been preached by the top coaches and practised by the top players. The funny thing is, they don't seem to work for me. At the end of the day, let's be honest and admit our failings. As the great Trevino says, 'You wake up with a slice? You play to a slice – aim further left.' Good advice in principle. But now O'Connor's First Law of Fairway Mechanics comes into play. Have you noticed how often, when you aim left to compensate for your slice, the ball flies straight and true into that thorn hedge beyond the left-hand rough? Now even your slice is letting you down, dammit!

So maybe it's better to turn to another technological wonder – the driver that has been produced to cure the slice? What ... straighten a slice?? Believe it or not, it's true. These drivers are not cheap, and some only vaguely resemble a conventional wood, but, by some law of physics, they compensate for a slice. So here's the slicer's dream come true – except for one small thing. The driver will happily play a straight tee shot, but what about my second shot, with fairway wood or long iron. What will straighten that out? And what about the 60-yard pitch that follows? Maybe I need a bag full of special clubs. How much will that cost? And what if, overnight, I lost the slice and found myself with a zillion pounds' worth of clubs that had nothing to compensate? Would they then give me a hook? What would I do then? Where would I aim my tee shot? I think I'll go and lie down for a minute.

When all's said and done, however, there are many simple, ungimmicky things that really can help to improve our game. The late great Henry Cotton extolled the virtues of using an old car tyre as a buffer to the club head when practising and in strengthening the left side, arm and wrist. To a similar end one can buy a specially weighted club, or a shaft with a weighted head. You can also buy, or make, wooden frames that can be placed on the floor (bedroom, kitchen, train corridor) and show you exactly where to place your feet in relation to the ball at address. Some have markings to show where in the stance you should place the ball for the driver, the 7 iron, and wedge. Who knows, improvement may come from such as this – though any sample of, say, 10 golfers of varying ability and age will show considerable differences in the location of the ball for use of, say, a fairway wood.

I'm sure it's merely my warped sense of humour, but all gadgets remind me of jokes:

CHARLIE: 'This hearing aid is the most sophisticated and delicately balanced piece of micro-technology in the history of audio-sonic research.'
HARRY: 'How much did it cost you?'
CHARLIE: 'Twenty past six!'

The cause of my apparent cynicism is actually two incidents in my own chequered experience of golf purchases.

The first involved the 'perfect tool for measuring

'It's in the rough. Three points to starboard, Fred.'

distance of ball to pin'. The brochure more or less invited me to do away with caddies and burn yardage carts. It was going to revolutionize my golf! All this enthusiastic waffle was about a small sextant-type implement which by the laws of geometry and trigonometry could determine by angles (and probably mirrors) the exact distance from one's ball to the hole, using readings and elevations to the top of the flag. What I didn't realize until after the first round was that the gadget assumed that *all* flags were of one particular height. (I can't to this day remember how far I actually flung the contraption.)

Embarrassment came to me a second time when confronted with the Mark 1 power-assisted golf trolley. Ah, I thought, leisure and pleasure: a fine walk with no weight on the shoulder. The booklet said: 'This battery is guaranteed to last one and a half rounds of golf [what a strange length of time], approximately 4.5 hours.'

I'm sure this statement was true, but it omitted an important rider, which should have read: *NB* In order not to appear a twit who has to push this 6 cwt cart for nine holes, make sure that when you stop for each shot you switch *off* the power.

Who left the power on? Who pushed that cart up hill and down dale for mile upon mile? It was – hang on a minute while I get my breath back – it was me, ex-smart alec. Me, back to normal: slightly below average golfer – taking the luck, taking the blows, but having fun.

But let's end this chapter on a positive note. There is one particular item of golfing equipment that will help to save you shots. I'm not referring to the 'hand mashie', 'leather niblick' or other non-kosher aid to extricating your ball from tiger country and other sloughs of despond. I'm talking about the Rules of Golf in a book form small enough to fit into one of the pockets of your golf bag.

You wouldn't play cricket seriously without understanding the laws of the game, especially those fairly technical ones relating to things like lbw and no-balls. And the same applies to other sports. Yet most weekend hackers like myself are serenely ignorant of the 'small print' in what is probably the most complex and wide-ranging set of rules of any outdoor sport. We amble round the 18 holes inter-preting the rules with greater or lesser liberality, depending on our mood, in a manner that would cause the R&A Rules of Golf Committee to chew the carpet.

All tournament pros know the rules backwards. But even they occasionally have to refer to one of the officially appointed referees for interpretation of some of the more complex ones. I think those of us who play purely for pleasure should give this wonderful game the respect it deserves and at least learn the more basic rules. Apart from anything else it will help us to get the better of some of the barrack-room lawyers who at present cow us with their apparent certainty of the rules – which, some-how, always seem to favour them rather than us!

At Royal Ascot we have a member who thinks he knows all the rules and is eager to demonstrate this at every opportunity. We call him Dracula because whenever his ball lands near a tree he shouts 'That's a stake.' To which we now bellow in unison 'No, it's a pork chop' and fall about.

3

Any Old Line for a Laugh!

TO PARAPHRASE Bill Shankly, 'Golf is like life except more serious.' Life is a series of highs, lows and in betweens. Sometimes it is not what it appears to be, and sometimes it is so cruel it makes us cry. But when life is good it is *so* good. Growing up is learning to live with *all* the quirks, surprises and pratfalls that life can throw at us.

Remember the teenage days in dance halls or discos? Remember the inane conversations with your pals?

> YOU: 'Boy, does that girl fancy me.'
> PAL: 'Really?'
> YOU: 'Definitely! I've already broken the ice with a belting line.'
> [Actually, it was 'Can I have the last dance with you?' Reply: 'You're having it!']
> PAL: 'What makes you so sure?'
> YOU: 'She started with "Get lost, creep" and clinched it with "I'm fed up, not hard up!" I'm telling you, she's mad about me.'

Sounds ridiculous now doesn't it? But compared

with the world of golf, that conversation is a beacon of logic and good sense.

WITNESS: 'I'd have birdied it if I hadn't five putted.'
(Oh yeah?)
'Everything in our favour was against us today.'
(Of course it was.)
'If we'd have played the first nine as well as the back nine we'd have only lost by two holes.'
(Eh?)

Enthusiasts who are capable of such remarks will believe anything, particularly if it's funny and happens to someone else.

Let me start with a story that I have checked out, and to the best of my knowledge is totally true. In Lancashire there is a golf course which features a massive electricity pylon just off the 14th fairway. There is a club rule regarding balls coming into contact with the overhead cables. (Ball, or its remains, to be replayed without penalty.) One morning a member entered the clubhouse swathed in plaster from shoulder to wrist, his fingers splayed on a metal plate, his neck in a surgical collar.

'My God,' said the steward, 'have you been in a car crash, Percy?'

'Worse, I played with Big Peter yesterday and he did this.'

'In a fit of rage?'

'In what he thought was an act of mercy.'

It appears that when the pair teed off from the fourteenth, Peter sliced his drive into the right rough – Indian country – near the pylon. In the ensuing search, Percy stepped into a marshy morass up to his shins – soaking his shoes, socks, trousers and legs in ooze. Without thought Percy leaned with left hand on the pylon whilst shaking his right foot vigorously. Big Peter, seeing the quivering foot and the position of his partner re the pylon, assumed that Percy was being electrocuted and, in an all-out effort to dislodge him, smashed him across the back with a four iron, breaking his shoulder.

True or not, this has the authentic golf story mix of the mundane and the wildly melodramatic. Golfers are romantics. We have a need to embellish and exaggerate our deeds – our failures just as much as our triumphs. Stretching the length of a successful putt by a factor of two or three is routine and perfectly acceptable. But the missed tap-ins are also wonderfully short: 'Couldn't have been more than five inches – a gimmie in anyone's book. The so-and-so made me putt out and in my anger I didn't allow for the wind.'

These and other lines never pass into obscurity because they are repeated, more or less word for word, by every generation of golfers. But there are some classics, like Arnold Palmer's remark after he had taken two shots to get out of a bunker in the Open: 'I'm not saying that God couldn't have got the first one out, but he'd have had to throw it.'

This story, of course, was recorded, witnessed and verified. Here's another that I can't absolutely vouch for, but, for those who know the parties involved, it has the ring of authenticity.

Fulford, the original home of the Benson & Hedges tournament (now played at St Mellion), is a super course in the super county of Yorkshire. And it was while playing in the B & H competition some years ago that I heard a marvellous story starring that

'All I said was, "Your friend Big Peter's here to see you."'

great character, Frederick S Truman. I've known Fred for a great many years and he has gone from my all-time cricket idol to becoming a great friend – a man who will give generously of time, talent and cash to a host of worthwhile charities, a man whose talent for story-telling is legendary. This is the tale of Fred at Fulford.

Arriving, as he sometimes does, in a flurry and only slightly late, Fred approached the head caddy saying: 'Now tha knows me, son, I want a good, reliable caddy.'

'Certainly, Mr Truman.'

'Call me Fred.'

'Right, Fred, we'll give you Bert. He's a cracker – he won't let you down.'

Bert duly appeared and was obviously the arche-typal caddy who'd been there and back and had the face to prove it.

'I'm your biggest fan, Mr Truman.'

'Call me Fred.'

The first at Fulford is a fairly straightforward hole, with only a modicum of trouble on the left to threaten a hacker's card. Fred launched a 2-wood at his ball, and to the delight of the gallery, struck it straight out of the screws. It travelled 280 yards, unluckily finishing in the rough on the left.

Without a by your leave, Bert was off like Linford Christie, the heels of his boots striking sparks from each other in his dash up the fairway. As Fred neared the rough he was amazed to see his ball pop out of the trouble and onto the fairway, followed by a grinning caddy:

'Bit of luck there, Mr Truman.'

'Call me Fred.'

Thinking silence was the best policy, Fred ambled up to the ball, stared at the green in the distance, and debated which club to use. Eventually, undecided, he turned to Bert: 'Would you say it was a 7-iron?'

Whereupon, Bert started scuffing the ball forward with his boot, saying 'Blimey, Fred, not yet!'

Golfing folklore is built on such tales. The acid test for a tale like this is not literal truth but truth to character and authenticity of feeling – the conviction that it *could* have happened, that it *ought* to have happened, and that, if it *did* happen, it would have been like this. It's then quite a short step for the storyteller at the 19th to claim not only that it actually happened but that he was a privileged onlooker, hero or victim of the incident. Every seasoned contributor to the club bar archive knows what to expect when the storyteller prefaces his latest fantasy by placing his hand on his heart and declaring 'As God is my witness ...', a form of words which apparently gives him licence to purvey the incredible.

Now, the interesting thing about this is that one of the reasons why golf is such a fertile ground for the fairway fantasists is because some very odd things really do occur on the golf course. The following story is absolutely true, as God is my ... erm – I mean honestly, I kid you not.

I was visiting a course located in the very rough outer suburbs of an industrial town in the north of England. In the changing rooms there was a dejected-looking hacker seated with head in hands. 'I just can't understand it,' he muttered. 'I don't know how to apologize.' I looked as sympathetic as

possible – he seemed a pleasant enough bloke – and asked him what was wrong. It seems that while on holiday abroad he had made friends with a hacker from the south of England who, on their return home, had invited him to his Sussex home for a golfing weekend at his club, the famous old Royal Eastbourne, where they spent many a pleasant hour in its elegant clubhouse.

Soon it was time for the return match, as it were, and his friend came up to play and sample the delights of northern hospitality.

'Can you believe it?' moaned my hacker. 'We reach the elbow on the dogleg seventh to be confronted by a crowd of yobs playing five-a-side football on the fairway. We had to play over them.'

'You're joking,' I said.

'You think that's bad? Wait till I tell you about the fourteenth. There was a burnt-out car in the greenside bunker! I mean, can you credit it? My friend was not very impressed, I can tell you. He's in the bar now. What the hell am I going to say to him?'

'Look,' I said, 'in golf the iron rule is to capitalize on good or bad strokes of luck. What you've got to do is convince your friend he's been lucky enough to experience something in golf that he's unlikely to come across ever again – and certainly not in the patrician environs of Royal Eastbourne. Just imagine what kind of reception he'll get from his fellow hackers at his home club when he tells them about it. "You'll never believe this," he'll say, "but when I was up north, as God is my witness...."'

Of course, the news of the outrages on the seventh and fourteenth had by now reached the ears of the club secretary and pro, and a little while later, as I was walking to the first tee, the assistant pro told me: 'We've broken up the five-a-side, but the car's still in the bunker. Treat it as an immovable obstruction and take a free drop – within the bunker, of course!'

Well, at least that was better than having to play the ball from inside the car – a fate even worse than that of the great Harry Bradshaw, who had to hit his ball out of a broken beer bottle in the 1949 Open. But hey! – what a story!

Most golfing tales feature players being lucky or unlucky, winning or losing – being the source of humour or the butt of it. Now and again it's nice to hear a tale of off-the-course humour where the good guy wins and the braggart bites the dust. So no apologies for a club steward anecdote that seems to me to be a classic of its kind.

A party of 12 loud, overweight American tourists arrived at a small, friendly golf club in the north. They spent the first hour making the customary tour of the clubhouse, bar and pro shop, making much noise and impressing no one. Then, attired in colours as subtle and aesthetically pleasing as the change strip of a Third Division club, they proceeded to subject the course to the sort of punishment usually associated with JCBs. Several dozen balls later the three groups of four returned, stripped and drained Lake Windermere whilst showering, before, smothered in Brut, they swaggered into the bar. Then, drinks ordered and half quaffed, they commandeered a table for lunch and studied the menu of bar meals and salads.

At this moment, the star of the story arrived in

the form of an old, grumpy waiter with a game leg and a legion of war tales. ('This is not a job to me, you know, pal ...') – we've all met him, most often as the night porter in a third-class hotel in Gateshead.

As the waiter was giving out the pats of butter to go with the bread rolls, the head American snapped his fingers and said: 'Hey, I always have two butters.'

'Listen, pal,' said our hero, 'club rules: one plate – one pat of butter.'

'But I always have two.'

'Watch my mouth, pal – one plate, one pat of butter.'

The American said, 'Do you know who I am?'

'You tell me,' our hero replied.

'I'm a multimillionaire, I've got businesses in 48 states. I've got a 200,000-acre ranch. I've got five oil wells.'

'And do you know who I am?' asked the waiter.

'No.'

'I'm the chap with the butter.'

In a perverse sort of way, folk like the waiter are my all-time heroes – people who say or do something so brilliant that you think, 'God, I wish I'd thought of that,' or 'One day I'll use that,' or 'If only I had the nerve!'

Over the years I've compiled a list of favourite 'one liners', like the man who rang the police station and said: 'I believe you caught the burglar who broke into our house last night?'

'Yes, sir,' said the sergeant.

'Could you ask him to tell you how he got in without waking the wife?'

While hosting a big TV variety show I witnessed one of the best one-line deflaters I've ever heard.

The show featured one of those smart-alec magicians who get volunteers to come up on stage and then make fools of them. Having chosen a little Yorkshire chap as victim, our star dragged him on stage and enquired: 'If I put my hand in your inside pocket and pulled out a rabbit, would you be surprised?'

'I'd be amazed,' replied the tyke, 'I've got a ferret in there!'

Oh, how I wished the show had been live – at least I would have proof of the story. In golf the quality of the story usually is proof enough. Perhaps it's because in golf we *want* to believe – in fact, we *demand* that all is truth if all is fun. Any old line for a laugh – as long as the laugh is not on us, hey?

Who wouldn't trade places with the golfer in mufti at the spikes bar of a rather swanky club who is approached by the club snob.

'I say, what are you doing here?'

'Actually I'm with a society – our annual "do"'.

'Oh, and do you have a club of your own?' asks snob.

'Yes, Huyton & Prescot – it's on Merseyside.'

'And is it a links course?'

'Yes, it links the east Lancashire road to the motorway.' (Fade lights and bow out snob.)

Sometimes of course the gods of golf can be unkind to the 'good guys', as they sometimes are to the accomplished player. Take the previous story with slight variation. Same bar, same couple, different opening gambit.

'You have a club of your own, I suppose?'

'Yes, it's up north.'

'And what sort of membership do you have?'

'Well, basically it's a fair cross section of the community.'

'Ah,' says snob, 'fortunately we don't have that problem here!'

(Which club would *you* nominate to have been the origin of the story?)

Being a golfer means being a party to the whims of fate, to peculiar remarks and strange conversations. I remember my mother, bless her, almost crying with laughter at the following exchange between two old ladies on a bus:

'How's Charlie now, then?'

'Oh, he's a lot better, but he still has to stand sideways.'

The mind boggles at Charlie's problem, but in my case it was quite simple. If you recall, I'd been felled by a golf ball, and, having been swathed in various items from the medicine chest and sleeping the sleep of the fed up, I was persuaded to 'get back on the horse' the next day. It was a charity Celebrity-Am at Patshull Park, near Wolverhampton, organized by my good friend and sparring partner Rachael Heyhoe Flint. The day was fine, the company even better. My team included a lovely lady who was not only a Curtis Cup player but also the daughter of George Willard, the man who had given me my first lesson long ago at Gorleston.

Because of my giddy spells and slightly blurred vision, I was delighted to have the services of a caddy, Sam, a single-figure handicapper and local golfer, to see me through. On the first I hit a nondescript sort of shot – a three wood, slightly open face, 220 yards, finishing in semi-rough on the right.

'Not bad,' said my addled brain. 'Twenty-four hours after a bad knock – you're lucky you can swing the club at all.' On reaching the ball, lying quite nicely, Sam assured me I could get 'very near the green' with a four wood 'well struck'.

As the God of golf is my witness I struck a four wood as hard as I ever have and the ball flew as if jet propelled.

'Great,' thought I, 'the land's back with the people' – until, only half-way through its flight, Sam shouted: 'Don't worry – it's not as bad as it looks.'

What a way to make a comeback – accompanied by the doyen of the understatement. But golf's like that, you win some, you lose some. You're never happy with a draw, and when disaster strikes do not fool yourself that things can't get any worse. They can, they can!

And then even your golfing pals start throwing clichés at you:

'There's always someone worse off than you.' (Yeah? Show me!)

'I had no shoes and complained, until I met a man who had no feet!' (But did *he* always shank with his 9-iron?)

Yes, there's always something to complain about, golfwise. But then, nobody really thinks golf is important, do they? Nobody lets it totally dominate their life, do they? Nobody gets so upset by their game that they even rant and rave at the dog if no one else is available, do they? Nobody thinks that grass is green and apples grow on trees, do they?

Well, there was the grizzled old hacker who was universally regarded as the club grouch – Mr Nasty himself. The story goes that, when he was finally laid to rest, these words were carved on his headstone:

Who Are You Looking At?

Hey, that's enough of this gloom. Let's go out of this chapter with a smile. In later chapters I'll be celebrating the names of some fine people who have helped spread the good name of golf by word, by deed and simply by being good and talented human beings. I would never dream of trying to place these people in any order of excellence – they all count as one to me. But the following story particularly involves a greatly talented entertainer, the late Dickie Henderson. He was a true professional, and an example of all that's best in show business and in life. He was kindness itself to me – a mere sprog-comic trying to learn how to do the job right.

I had been booked for a three-week stint at the Savoy Grill in London. This was good news and bad news. It was a glamorous venue all right; but it had the reputation of being difficult to work – it was often full of foreigners or of people interested only in talking among themselves. In short, a comic's graveyard. What to do? First off, I made it a condition of the contract that before my stint I would have the opportunity to watch another 'talker' work the room. It turned out that no such 'talkers' had been booked for the immediate future before I was due to appear. But then I was told that Dickie Henderson had offered to do a stand-up patter act just for me. And he did. Although he omitted some of the real gems of his act, he stormed the room – standing ovation, prolonged applause, but nothing was more fervent than the glow of gratitude in my young, spellbound eyes.

I'll always remember Dickie. And I shall continue to pass around one of the classic true stories associated with him. You remember, Dickie – the one about the cab ride? The occasion was a big charity golf match held at one of the major London clubs in the summer of 1962. Golfers and celebrities from all over Britain and beyond would be appearing. Dickie had arranged to travel to the club with three other celebrities – Bruce Forsyth, Ronnie Carroll, the fine Irish singer and a talented sportsman, and Sean Connery, who never takes prisoners at golf.

They decided to go by cab and Bruce ('I'm in charge!') took it upon himself to hail one. A passing taxi was whistled down and Dickie, Ronnie and Sean got into the back, while Bruce issued instructions to the driver:

'There's 30 bob extra if you put your foot down. I'll explain the route as we go.'

The cabbie looked him over. 'I know you, don't I?'

'Never mind that,' said Bruce, 'let's get going.'

'But I've seen you before – I know I have.'

'Come on, old son, we're in a hurry.'

'Where have I seen your face? Is it off the telly?'

'Yes.'

'Who are you, then?'

'I'm Bruce Forsyth.'

'Oh yeah – and I'm James Bond!'

Whereupon there was a tap on the driver's shoulder and from the back seat Connery sternly announced:

'No, *I'm* James Bond!'

And can you imagine the scene later at one of

the taxi-drivers' cafés, with our cabbie trying to convince his pals? It's the 19th hole syndrome all over again:

'No, listen, lads – as God is my witness ...'.

4

Behind Every Successful Club Golfer There's a Very Surprised Wife!

THEY SAY that friends are friends because you can choose them but family are family because you're stuck with them. That may be so, but it always seems a biased argument to me. In fact a selfishly biased argument. If we are stuck with the family, they are stuck with us – and if we're golfers, they are stuck with more than the Good Lord intended. Isn't it a special relative who can bear our moods and rages and idiosyncrasies and still admit to being of the same stock? Aren't we the luckiest breed of humans – the select few whose family ties survive the most acid of tests: that of the non-golfer being backed into a corner and forced to listen admiringly to a blow-by-blow account of dad's latest bout of derring-do (or, more likely, derring-don't) on the links.

As a mere golfing husband, let me first of all write in praise of golfing wives and golfing widows – those ladies who would rather laugh at our oldest joke than laugh at our latest mistake. My Pat, the boss, is a golfing enigma. She has the best swing I've ever seen – simple, compact, rhythmic – but she won't play! I have been blessed with a spouse who has 'the gift', but 'can't be bothered'. For years I have mused over her reasoning. How can a person be put off golf because it is time consuming and requires too much concentration, and yet spend hours knitting everything from scarves to sweaters and bootees? Worthwhile end products, I grant you, if well made. (Which reminds me of that story about the husband trying on the cardigan. 'It feels fine,' he says, 'but the neck feels tight.' His wife replies: 'Relax, you've got your head through a buttonhole.')

But I digress. Pat is the loveliest of all people, intelligent, witty and extremely tolerant – which is just as well when you consider the liberties I take in the name of golf. It didn't take long for me to realize that the lounge of our house is ideal for practice. Its dimensions are such that I can swing any club, including my driver, and hit plastic airtex balls against a curtained wall. How Pat has coped with seven years of that I don't know. Now it's even worse with three grandchildren – each with their own club – practising with me. The odds on the carpet lasting the year out are millions to one, even if we *are* meticulous in replacing the divots.

What I've only just started to consider is the picture presented to visitors to our house who are invited into the lounge, regaled with tea, cake and chat and suddenly find themselves sitting in a mini-driving range as one or other of the family warms up before going out for a knock.

My dad, 80-plus, has even worked out a specific place to sit in the lounge where he is out of the

The Lounge Warm-Up

range of any club but can still see the TV perfectly.
I suggested that this sophisticated exercise in
geometry was worthy of a course at the Open Uni-
versity, but then my dad is a bit special. Ex-Liver-
pool docker, an extremely hard worker (he claims
he was the only docker with a straight hook!), good
provider, war veteran and the ultimate armchair
sportsman.

I well recall the 1980 Olympic games on TV. At
the time, my dad was 22 stones in weight and could
demolish 10 pounds of spuds in rapid time. There
he lay on the couch in front of the TV, a case of
Guinness on his right, a box of Woodbines on his
left – 22 stones clad in vest and braces watching the
pole vault and insisting: 'Gor blimey, I could do
better meself.' He's never played golf in his life, but
with that kind of confidence he could have done
well.

The game affects different members of the family
in different ways. In our case, Pat has the ability
but not the inclination. Our two younger daughters,
Frances and Helen, have good swings and could
play a steady game if they took time to practise.
Stephen, my son, a very good all-round sportsman,
is the one who has kept in touch with golf since his
younger days and plays a good-ish if power-packed
round. With the vigour of youth, Stephen has to hit
every ball as hard as possible and delicacy is the
short suit in his hand.

This can, if harnessed, be a major asset when
playing him for money! The secret is to have num-
bered covers on all the clubs including irons, but to
assign the numbers to the wrong clubs. So when he
sees me remove a 7-iron cover, he is happy to take

an 8- or even 9-iron to show his power. Of course, my 7-iron cover has been on a 5-iron! Devious – but permissible in the broad canvas of life that is golf. All is fair in love and war, but in golf there are many shades of fair depending on what is involved. Pride, money, trophies, peace of mind – they all are reasons why people play. Stretching their strength, skill and the rules to the limit.

But, oh the joy when all the effort is rewarded, when your best-laid plans succeed. A pal of mine, Eric, has devised (so he says) the foolproof method of staying late at the 19th without *reproof* from the good lady when he returns. Before he leaves home to go to the club competition he bets his wife £5 he'll be in before midnight. So when he returns at 2 am she's so delighted to win the bet she isn't bothered about the time. (I'm not sure this would work for me – but to be safe I'm not even going to try!)

I suppose I'm lucky regarding golf days and competitions, inasmuch as Pat quite enjoys going alone and chatting with the other ladies. Generally if it's a Celebrity-Am she'll have plenty of pals there and usually a buggy to whizz her around the course just to keep in touch with play. It's good to know she's thereabouts to lend support if and when I need it. And support was never more needed than at my first Pro-Celebrity event on television. In less than 24 hours, Pat was all at once my inspiration, my consolation, my irritation and my jubilation. Let me set the scene.

Turnberry on a very wet and exceedingly windy morning is not the ideal setting for a TV show of any kind. When it's an occasion calling not for showbiz knowhow but golfing ability, it becomes even more of a tester. I was of course delighted to be asked to play in the competition, partnering Sandy Lyle at his 1-iron best against the great Lee Trevino and my showbiz hero Jimmy Tarbuck. A better four-ball you couldn't wish to be in!

But I faced the same quandary as the Jewish guy who saw the sign 'Pork pies – half price' (good news and bad, see). For me the bad news was TV cameras analysing my swing, and a live gallery (albeit whittled down by the weather) of experts following us around. So with mixed feelings and my lovely Pat as support I managed to scramble my way through nine holes – leaving all the golf to Sandy but very occasionally getting in a 'funny' to justify my being there.

Three soggy hours later, thawing out at the 19th, I was approached by one of the organizers, who mentioned a special dinner to be held in honour of Tarby in Glasgow the following night.

'Would you come along and maybe say a few words?'

'Would I? Try and stop me, pal. It will be a pleasure.'

The next day dawned (surprisingly more sunny and certainly better for golf), and Pat and I found ourselves in a car with Ronnie Corbett bound for Glasgow. It turned out that quite a few 'faces' were making their way to the 'do' – all proceeds in aid of the Variety Club of Great Britain.

We arrived, we thought, in good time, only to be greeted by an extremely red-faced man who bellowed 'You're late!!'

'Is Michael Parkinson here yet?' enquired Ronnie Corbett.

'No.'

'Then he's the one who's late.'

This seemed to make some kind of Celtic sense and red face left to bellow at someone else.

Having showered, shaved and suited, I joined Pat in the queue of celebrities being marshalled by red face, who proceeded to call the roll:

'Parkinson, Mr and Mrs?' 'Here.'

'Connor, O, and Mrs?' 'Here.' (I figured he meant me).

'Seven Connery?' 'Here.' (Could that have been a Freudian slip? – NO.)

The meal went better than the line up and the audience were regaled with humour from Max Boyce, Kevin Keegan, Parky and many others, and the evening developed into a good, old-fashioned get-together – albeit with about a thousand guests. Time goes quickly when you're enjoying yourself and I certainly was. At one point I was at the bar with Sean Connery, Ronnie Corbett, Kevin Keegan and a man named Hughie, who had a chain of one butcher's shop. In the distance was the faint sound of an auction – '£300 I'm bid. Do I hear four? Four. Do I hear four fifty?'

'They're auctioning Jimmy Tarbuck's golf bag for charity,' said Ronnie.

'Who's the one upping the money?'

'Looks like your missus, Tom.'

'Six hundred I'm bid – six hundred from the lady in red. No more offers? Sold!'

Too late! – I was half-way to Pat's side travelling at the speed of light when the gavel fell.

'Give it back and auction it again,' I heard Pat say.

Behind every successful club golfer ...

'Can I have your autograph Mr O'Connor?'

'She's out of her mind,' I spluttered, 'it's a family trait at auctions.'

Anyway, I gladly paid up, but was now left with a super golf bag featuring Tarby's name and donated by Taylor Made. Unfortunately, I had to fly home to Heathrow and it meant standing at the carousel and collecting the bag I had taken to Turnberry, plus the bag that Taylor Made had given me (with *my* name on!), and Tarby's bag.

Carrying three full-size golf bags with dignity should be included in the Olympics. In my case the pain was tempered by bumping into the lovely, much lamented Roy Kinnear, who grinned and said: 'Taken it up full time, have you?'

Thanks Roy, and thanks Pat. Jimmy's bag raised £750 at a charity auction in Liverpool two months later.

I have a happy ending, and isn't that what golf gives us? I mean, if we play brilliantly, our mouths go into overdrive and the world never hears the end of it. If we play badly, our brains go into overkill and make it the *worst* round the world has ever seen:

'Four-putted ten greens.'

'Shanked six wedge shots.'

'Topped every drive except the first – that was an air shot.'

What a game!

5

'I've Signed Up with an International Agent, So Now I'm Out of Work All Over the World!'

AS I WRITE this chapter I'm propped up in bed early in the morning in a Harrogate hotel, frantically trying to find a place to sleep tonight! Let me explain. It's all to do with the tricky business of combining my professional career with my prime passion – golf!

I've always maintained, and heard very little contrary argument, that golf is best played with a clear head and a body at least half rested. If I've arranged to have a round I like if possible to have a restful evening before. Easy to say, but, with my lifestyle, damned difficult to achieve at the best of times.

My present problem concerns an after-dinner speech in Harrogate tonight at 11pm, a drive through the night to dodge the traffic, a place to lay my head for a couple of hours, and a 9.30am tee off time in a charity game in Romford. Why Romford? Why such a tight schedule? Why think you can play a decent game after that punishing drive? Why? – 'cos, like Everest, it's there. So why not? If we want to suffer the slings, arrows, brickbats, name-calling and all round bad humour, whose business is it except ours? To those who are not in the grip of the golfing curse, we may appear to be daft masochistics. On the contrary, we are a higher form of existence who realize that the finer part of living requires not a little effort and suffering, especially suffering.

How can we explain our philosophy to the unconverted and partly washed? Any fool knows that the beauty of banging your head against a brick wall is the feeling of relief when you stop. Likewise, the misery of a freezing cold, rain soaked 18 holes of air shots, duffs, shanks and triple bogeys is beautifully eased by a warm fire, a large brandy and a load of lies at the 19th hole. To the non-golfer this may not seem to be very sensible. But who wants to base his life totally on good sense? As the man said, 'A pal of mine has just given up drinking, smoking, overeating and staying out all night. Poor fellow. In 30 years' time he'll be lying in bed dying of nothing!'

Was he the same man who bought shoes three sizes too small? When asked why, he said, 'In the last 12 months my wife's left me, my business has gone bust, my car's been repossessed and my house has burned down. Now the only pleasure I get in life is when I take these shoes off.'

Now any golfer can sympathize with these emotions. Any golfer knows that to suffer and fail is much better than not to bother at all.

Hence the problem I have right this minute: where to stay if all the hotels around Romford are full? Consolation comes from the knowledge that I am not alone. Throughout the world at this instant there are thousands, maybe millions, of men and women like me trying to organize tomorrow's round, willing to snatch a bit of shut-eye in club car parks in order to get to the tee on time. And members of clubs are lucky – what about the faithful who get in the queue outside the pro shop at public courses well before dawn in order to play a round that may take 5 hours and more to complete?

I sometimes get this picture of St Peter at Heaven's gate talking to three lately departed spirits in plus fours: 'You can't go out as a three, but just hang on a moment – there's a decrepit old wrinkly trying to negotiate Cardiac Hill at Torquay!'

Talking of saints, who would you nominate to be the patron saint of golf? There are plenty of suitable candidates. St Andrew would be an obvious and appropriate choice. Or might it be St Antony, who is renowned for finding things (including lost balls?) What about St Jude, the patron saint of hopeless cases? Then there's St Nicholas (spelt 'Nicklaus'). My suggestion would be St Christopher, who cares for travellers – and who travels further, on and off the course, in pursuit of his hobby than a golfer?

Most of us, heaven knows, could do with saintly assistance on the golf course. Oh, I know that in golf all people are equal because of the handicap system (though most of us suffer at the hands of bandits from time to time). In theory, Joe, a 28 handicapper, could give Woosie a game. In fact, two golfers with the same (genuine) handicap may play each other every day for a week and have wildly fluctuating results over the seven days. For all but the finest players – and even for some of them – consistency of performance is impossible. It is

'Antony, mate! You're just the bloke.'

because occasionally, during the course of a round, things go absolutely to plan that golf for the hacker becomes an obsession, a thing of burning passion.

Golf delights me not only as a game but as a social phenomenon. Forget, for a moment, those snooty clubs that continue to be obsessed with class and gender. The fact is, on the course and at the 19th hole, men and women, young and old, are equal. The only other place I experience this is in hotels.

Hotels? Yes, those places where, out of need, we must lay the weary head and hope for several hours' undisturbed sleep before we play for a big side bet, a worthwhile charity or the town hall clock. Hotels and their machinations can actually spark off more conversations than the weather. I said hotels treat people as equals. I did not say they treat them well. My first intimation that staying even in first-class hotels might not be entirely blissful came not in Britain but in beautiful Australia.

Of all the places in the world I have been – and thanks to my work I've been to most – my all-time favourite city is Sydney. The harbour, the Opera House, the Henry 9th pub, the Irish Drovers. But mostly the people. In Sydney I found a vibrant population, young-thinking (no matter what age they were), go-getting – still going forward and enjoying life. It's like the 60s are still happening and the world is just a tad younger.

I have fond memories of my first visit: we flew out from London to join the *Canberra* for a three-week leg of its world cruise. It's a long flight – 'double jet lag', Pat calls it – about 20 odd hours and God knows how many time zones. We flew from drizzly Heathrow, via humid Singapore, to baking hot

Sydney. Shattered, we checked into our hotel, hardly having the energy to take in the sights during the taxi ride. The hotel receptionist said: 'Mr O'Connor? One moment, sir – a message for you.'

A message for me – from whom? Perhaps an ex-pupil of mine or Pat's, perhaps an exiled Scouser who'd bought one of my comedy tapes, perhaps someone I owed a few bob? Wrong! It was a welcome note from two great personal friends, Danny La Rue and Ray Allen (not forgetting Lord Charles). They were in the gaff next door. They realized we'd be too tired to join them that night, but could they give us some advice? No matter how tired we were at 5.30pm we were not to go to bed until the normal time, say 11pm. That way, we would sleep our way through the jet lag. 'Get a few gins down you,' they urged, 'and keep those eyes open!' Good advice at the time, but then who knows what can happen in the course of a night?

The concierge recommended a quiet little water-hole next door – the Henry 9th Bar! Here, Pat and I stood in the street, drank pints of Guinness actually brought out to us, and thrilled to the sounds of the Irish Drovers, a great band of exiled Irishmen who filled the pub to overflowing and sang every Irish song ever written. (Three years later I returned to that bar and met Myles Mooney and the boys and 'shifted a few' with them – ah! but that's another tale.)

Suitably awash with Guinness we retired to our hotel room for the night. 11.30pm – just right. 'Do not disturb' sign on the door. Quick glance at the telly. Not a good idea! On came an advert giving advice on what to do if bitten by a funnel-web spider – no known antidote, hangs out in loos and dark places. Keep the lights on. If bitten, keep still so the poison doesn't spread quickly. (Why bother if there's no known cure?)

Thanks to the funnel-web, I was still awake in a room bathed in light at 3.00am. But then, the Lord be praised, I must have drifted off because the next thing I knew the bedroom door was bursting open. No, not a giant spider, but a very large Australian lady bearing a tray with a steaming mug.

'Tea,' she drawled forcing the tray upon me.

'But it's only six o'clock,' I protested, 'and I put do not disturb on the door....'

'Tea,' she drawled again.

There I sat, tray on my lap, as she pounded to the door, where she turned: 'Do you take sugar?'

'Er – no.'

'Then don't stir it.'

Welcome to the bizarre world of the hotel.

The logistics and modus operandi of most hotels are in many respects totally at variance to the needs of their customers. How come a place where most people spend the night and early morning is managed by a person who knocks off in the early evening? How come, no matter at what time you arrive on a cold winter's evening, the night porter is always on his fire round? How come a 'do not disturb' sign inspires chambermaids to acts of outrage?

Let's start with the sign. Obviously the day staff have no idea what time you arrived in the night, or how tired you are, or whether you have to play the game of your life tomorrow. What they *do* know is

'Tea up, sport!'

that if Elsie doesn't get you up and out then she won't be able to clock off with the others. So 'do not disturb' is less an instruction than a challenge.

It usually starts at about 7.00am, when the door opens just a crack and a voice says 'Oops – sorry!" – that's the opening salvo. At 7.15 there's a rap on the door with the butt end of a key and a shouted 'Check your mini bar?' (Funny, you never noticed one last night.)

'Er – I didn't use it.'

'Thank you.'

Now they've got you semi-awake, the trick is to play on your nerves until you decide it would be more peaceful to get out and go and stand on a traffic island in the middle of the rush hour.

So in all the rooms around yours – that's five in all – they turn on the radios, tune each to a different station, and turn the volume up to full blast. I once asked a manager why they did this. Believe it or not, the official reason is so that the housekeeper knows where each maid is at any time!

Next comes the Hoover in the corridor outside your room and the bellowed conversation down the hallway.

'Have you done the two in the corner?'

'Yes, I've done all this side except for one.'

Now here's why we are all equal no matter what our age, sex, colour or creed: '127's still resisting!!'

So that's what you are: a number, an object occupying the wrong piece of space – a pain in the neck for Elsie and the girls!

In the restaurant you're a comestible: 'He's the prawn and she's the crab with the frogs' legs.' As a person, you appear to have lost all individuality –

except in the eyes of the night porter. All praise to the one shining light in the residents' darkness. The man who lets you know, often at inordinate length, that he's been there, done that, fought every foe, suffered every affliction, undergone unbearable pain, and could run this hotel standing on his head given the chance. Eh? Oh no, he can't make you a cheese sandwich – he's forgotten the combination of the fridge.

We've all had run-ins with this guy. He's in every hotel in every city in the world, and he's at his most awkward when you are most desperate. Let me tell you my classic tale – verified by my wife and a night porter called Quentin (truly!) The location of the hotel has been altered for reasons which will become obvious.

It was summer and I had done a show at the North Pier in Blackpool. I had finished at 11.15pm and was driving through the night to Great Yarmouth to play in a shot-gun start charity game. It's a long run, possibly five hours, so Pat suggested we ring up a hotel en route to see if they had a room.

Using the car phone I got through to a place near Norwich and, yes, they had a suite to spare. The lounge had been used that evening for a conference but the bedroom was unused: room 216. We arrived at about 3.00am and were greeted by Quentin. 'Just caught me – a minute later I'd have been on my fire round.' He gave us the key to 216: 'It's just down there. You can manage your own luggage, can't you? – it's me war wound, you see.'

Pat and I dragged the bags to the suite, opened the door and found the lounge unkempt but OK. What we didn't know was that a day porter, who

knew the room was vacant, had chatted up a wait-
ress and they were in bed next door! All in one
movement I opened the bedroom door and put on
the light. Before me was a scene of the utmost
embarrassment. To say the least, the couple were in
a totally compromising position and suffice to say
that he was looking up! As our eyes met, I snapped
off the light and closed the door. I turned to Pat
and remarked that for the rest of his life, when
asked if the earth ever moved for him, he was going
to say 'No – but now and again I see Tom O'Connor!'

Well, that's fame for you!

'No, the earth didn't move for me but I did get a flash of Des
O'Connor – or was it Tom?'

6

'The Audience Were With Me All the Way. I Finally Shook Them Off at the Railway Station'

OF COURSE, not all journeys in pursuit of golf are disasters. I'm sure you, like me, have had great golfing times – magic moments, unforgettable meetings, wonderful courses. And maybe, like me, you try to combine in your imagination the best points from each club so as to build a picture of the ideal place to golf your life away.

Let's start with Ireland – home of the lovely folk – where life is still a little come day, go day, and where what they say isn't always what they mean:

'Follow me, I'm right behind you.'

'Spread out in a bunch.'

'Single file in twos.'

I was over in Dublin recently doing cabaret work and had a chance to play Portmarnock golf club with my good friend Commandant Joe O'Keefe whose excellent short game saved us £5 each. What a great day on a great course, where the world goes away for four hours and then the whole history of golf and golfing greats comes rushing back when taking Guinness and sandwiches in the clubhouse. Thanks for the day, Joe. Yes, I'll be back soon. Next time I'll also re-visit St Margaret's, a new golf complex near Dublin airport. Super clubhouse, a very promising course and excellent staff. Why, the steward was even waiting at the 10th tee with a round of drinks – he'd remembered what we'd ordered earlier on, including the half pint of Guinness with blackcurrant in it for Tommy, my manager (a peculiar chap: worst swing in the world, no sense of direction, no timing, no hope – but a good talker – the most important gift in my golfing circles).

It was while talking at the bar in St Margaret's that I was privileged to hear the ultimate in Irish stories. (I know I promised not to tell any more, so here's the first of them.) Two high handicappers are wiring into their ninth or tenth beverage when one says: 'I'm thinking of whitewashing the shed, you know.'

'Oh really. And what colour were you thinking of whitewashing it?'

'Well, I was going to whitewash it green.'

'Listen, let my son do it for you. He'll whitewash it any colour you like, it won't cost you a penny and it'll be a few bob for the boy.'

Who said the Irish aren't logical people? And I would have them round me on any golf day anywhere, any weather. They bring a smile wherever they go and a smile brightens even the darkest day. Talking of which, golf in Ireland is usually played in the rain. If you love playing there – and who doesn't? – but like to keep dry, consult the goats of Lahinch. This wonderful links on the coast of County Clare has long been home to goats, who graze the rough and dunes. Whenever a storm is on the way they infallibly make for the lee of the club house. They are so reliable that a sign, 'See goats', was attached to a long-defunct barometer inside the club house.

So for our ideal golf day we'll need to have the fun and the logic of the Emerald Isle. Then we must take the wit of Merseyside so that we can laugh at any misfortune that befalls us. The lovely Arthur Askey was convinced that Scousers laughed at things to show they weren't afraid of them. Could be true – but what a strange sense of humour. Take the broken-hearted club member sobbing his heart out at the 19th:

'What's up, Frank?' asks the steward.

'What's up? What's up? The end of my world, mate. The end of my world.'

'Come on, it can't be that bad, Frank.'

'Can't be that bad! Can't be that bad! Let me tell you my day today. I got home from night work at seven this morning. There's a note from the wife – she's left me and run off with the milkman. The two boys have run away to join the Moonies, the car's been pinched and I've just got knocked out of the Captain's Cup. I can't understand it – I was two up at the turn!'

What else would we have on an ideal day? What about the irrepressible vigour of youth? The bold and aggressive way the young approach golf. The carefree flowing swing, the constant urge to practise till palms bleed, the readiness to accept advice, criticism and praise with grace and good humour. Wide eyed, their world is as yet undiscovered. It unfolds day by day and every day is Christmas. So much to learn, so much to remember, so many new

'Look out Charlie. It's going to ram, I think!'

shots to practise. So many golf stories to listen to – and then pass on to their pals.

Of course, youth often causes confusion with its innocence and honesty. I was playing in the Howard Keel Golf Classic at Mere golf club, near Manchester – a wonderful charity event and always with a terrific cabaret in the evening. As usual there were celebrities from all over the world – Vic Damone, Tony Christie, Robert Powell, Bruce Forsyth, Jeremy Kemp, Eddie Large and many, many more.

In the early years of the event the youngsters in the gallery would dash all over the course trying to get all the celebrities' autographs in the minimum time. Now they've learned. The bulk of the youngsters wait on the 18th green, that way ensuring that they catch all the stars and – who knows? – maybe cadge a souvenir ball.

On this occasion, after a reasonable round, I strode onto the 18th green. I was garishly clad in bright red and sporting a Greg Norman straw hat. Obviously the star turn. However, disillusion was at hand. After putting out I was approached by a youngster. 'Sign this, please.'

Taking her programme, I wrote 'Best wishes, Tom O'Connor'. The youngster looked at it and shouted to her friend, 'It's not him!' To this day, I don't know who I was supposed to be! Never mind, who cares? Youth must have its day and youth must be with us on our ideal golf day.

What's that I hear you cry? You want to play under warm, cloudless skies? In that case, regrettably, we'd have to look abroad. I say 'regrettably' because, when the sun *does* shine here at home you wouldn't want to be anywhere else for your golf. For guaranteed fine weather, however, we must go elsewhere – but where?

Let me confess at once that a lover of the sun I am not. I'm the guy you see after two hours' sunbathing walking like a crab and saying 'Don't touch me – bring the calamine!' I never get bronzed. My usual maximum is two or three interconnected freckles. Consequently, there are many wonderful golfing spots which may not essentially be my ideal.

I was lucky enough to enjoy a working holiday on the beautiful island of Barbados. It simply involved a couple of cabaret spots and introducing a steel band. No problem. Pat and I stayed at the Colony Club, a marvellous set-up where dwell experts on all matters Caribbean. (This expertise included how to treat a sting from a sea urchin. I *think* it involved the use of vinegar and candle wax.)

At the time of year we visited, the weather consisted of 10 minutes of torrential early rain and blinding sunshine for the rest of the day. This was perfect for Pat's hobby of lying under a baking sun sipping fruit cocktails. Me? I would spend a few minutes in the shade covered in factor 15 and then repair to an air-conditioned bar.

Oh yes, I was tempted out on a 'pirate' ship, the *Captain Patch*. Aboard there was a sumptuous barbecue, plenty of rum, and a crowd of Geordies who somehow seemed out of place singing a reggae version of 'Blaydon Races'. This was in addition to scuba diving and snorkelling in beautiful clear water inhabited by the most brilliantly coloured fish I've ever seen. It was like swimming through a kaleidoscope. Yes, a super day – marred only by the fact that I virtually got sunstroke before Pat realized that the barrier cream I was smearing all over me was actually aftersun!

But back to business. It's a beautiful place to holiday, but what about the golf? Well, I quickly found a picturesque course at St James's and learned essential lessons about Caribbean conditions. Number one, there seems to be no resistance in the air: the ball flies so much further, it's hard to choose the right club to play. The first at St James's was about 304 yards according to the card but I drove the green with a 3-wood, then cleared the green again when gently pitching back with my sand wedge. It took several days to adjust to this – but it proved invaluable when playing for money against new arrivals. Another lesson I quickly learned was that the only way I could play a full round was to begin at 6am and finish before the heat became overpowering.

So the Caribbean offers exotic food – including my favourite swordfish – rum, reggae and calypso, a guaranteed 10 minutes only of rain and no wind resistance. Where can we take them to make up the complete golfing weather? For me it has to be Spain. I will probably have plenty of supporters and possibly the odd critic for this choice, but let me explain my reasons.

To start with, every trip to España has been for me a thoroughly relaxing and enjoyable time. Let me tell you about Marbella. I'd been booked for three nights' cabaret at a super complex called Miraflores and worked to capacity business each night. By way of celebration, Pat decided we should move along the coast and spend the rest of the week at Puerto Banus, just taking the air. This led to the most amazing day of my life. We rented a flat above a block of shops right by the security barrier at the port, and spent the first night visiting all the piano bars and admiring all the yachts with their colour-coordinated Rolls-Royces. Finally we hit the sack about 5.30am, expecting to have little sleep and to be awakened by the morning bustle.

Guess what – no bustle! No noise till about 11am. Shangri-la (or possibly sangria-la!) Full of the joys of the partially rested, we strolled to the nearest café for a full English breakfast. Surprise number two! The café had just been bought by a man who had lost his job as a journalist in the Wapping episode and we were his first customers. So the breakfast, and two large gins, were on the house. Strolling towards the security barrier we were accosted by a young chap hawking timeshares. 'Obviously a person like you wouldn't want one, but would you just turn up at the site and say I sent you?'

Anything to oblige, especially after a free scoff. Surprise number three: the timeshare people were looking for a celebrity to lend his name to the publicity for the complex, and in return he could have a free three-bedroomed timeshare for one week per year. Having checked that the whole operation was kosher (it was, and still is today), I gladly supported the scheme and by 1pm was the owner of a timeshare.

Celebrating over a cool beer, I got talking to a British emigré who had recalled seeing me on TV and was a big fan of *Name That Tune*. Did I have a car? Yes, I'd rented one but I found it difficult to park. As a property developer in the port, could he offer me a key to an underground air-conditioned car park? He certainly could: surprise number four!

After another celebratory beer I thought it wise to take a taxi to the golf club. The Aloha is a beautiful course with a super clubhouse – home of many happy memories for me. Nights of fun with Kenny Lynch and Toni Dali; great golf days featuring Ted Dexter, Kevin Keegan and many others. But also the cause of surprise number five.

Grabbing a bucket of balls I wandered out to the practice ground and began knocking a few off. Along came the pro who watched a couple of shots and then proceeded, free of charge, to correct a minor fault in my swing. Wow! Only 2.30pm and five lucky breaks already! Could I find a horse to back? Or a pools coupon to fill out? 'Cos today's my lucky day! Marbella, I love you.

Marbella is a jewel of Spain, like Seve, Manuel, José-Maria (both), José solo – all wonderful players who have done the Ryder Cup proud over the years. Surely Spain must host it soon? It has so many courses where perfection is the norm and good company is guaranteed. We each have our favourites and I would not wish to influence any choice, but as a family favourite the O'Connors would have to opt for La Manga club.

There's a scene in the movie *The Magnificent Seven* when Yul Brynner is approached by the villagers to help them fight bandits, and they offer him all their watches and jewellery. 'In my time I've been offered much,' says Yul, 'but never everything.' At La Manga club we got everything. Let me expand.

In the course of making a golfing video to

accompany *From the Wood to the Tees* and this book,
we approached my good friend Rachael Heyhoe
Flint as to the possibility of using her connections
with La Manga. What a break! My manager Tommy,
Pat and I were promised the warmest of welcomes
when we flew out with a film crew, and so it was to
be. After a pleasant flight we were met by the man
from the car hire firm. Tommy produced his licence
and ID, signed the necessary forms, paid the fee –
and then gave me the keys.

'I can't drive on the wrong side of the road,' he
explained. 'You'll have to do it. Anyway, you've
been to Spain before so you know your way around.'
So, taking a quick mental refresher course on left-
hand drive, right-hand side of the road, I eased us
out of the airport, leaving a gob-smacked rental
chap.

I'd been to La Manga some years before as part
of a tour of one-night stands and had never really
appreciated its full worth. But now was different.
The warmest of welcomes started when we met Chris
Davies, my favourite Welshman. He's a good single-
figure golfer, a great teller of ribald tales (if you
ever meet him ask him to tell you about being
booked by the traffic warden in south Wales!) and
was soon to become a close friend. Chris helped us
move into a very plush apartment and gave us a
rundown of the various restaurants, sports facilities
and general amenities. Our plan was to stay a week
and already I realized we wouldn't have time to do
half the things we wanted to.

The crew arrived next morning and we formed
our plans at a meeting with boss of leisure Keith
Raynor, John Weir (a great golf pro and teacher)

and Chris Davies. We'd play a round of nine holes on the La Princessa course, filming shots, comic asides and staged gags, then do a cabaret in the clubhouse involving anecdotes (true and otherwise) and finally film a selection of gadgets that claim to lower one's handicap. This was all to take place the following day. Meantime, while Chris and the crew did a recce, Pat, Tommy and I decided on a leisurely drive to see the local sights.

Our prime need was for English newspapers and we were recommended to try the nearby town of Los Bolones. What a place! Don't ever be told that only the Irish are illogical: visit Los Bolones on a shopping spree. Whatever you need you can probably get – but not where you'd expect to buy it. We had to go to the chemist shop for newspapers; Tommy got his cigarettes in the electrical store and, unbelievably, the only place that sold bread and cakes was the garage. God knows where you'd go for petrol – the vets, maybe? The town itself was so quiet I doubt we saw a dozen people including shopkeepers – reminding me of the old joke about the town being so small that the local fire brigade was a four-year-old bedwetter.

The place that really stunned me was the furniture store. It contained pianos, three-piece suites, 12-seater dining tables – and yet there wasn't a house for miles around that was big enough to hold any of these. Maybe they were there only as a front and the shop really sold meat pies.

We joked about it that evening over a superb fish meal. We sat enthralled by the banter of Chris and company, and I tried to compete in the story telling. Fortunately, like me, they enjoy Jewish humour so

'Gippy tummy, señor? You go see Pedro the plumber, pronto.
No problem.'

I was able to press a recall button and rattle out my favourites.

Jewish lady at a play suddenly calls out:

'Is there a doctor in the house?'

'I'm a doctor, madam.'

'Have I got a daughter for you!'

Same Jewish lady to stranger at the bar:

'You look like my third husband.'

'Oh, and how many times have you been married?'

'Twice.'

The one that tickled Chris was the story that could have happened anywhere I suppose, but as a Jewish tale it works for me. A local man had died and the new rabbi had been asked to conduct a memorial service.

'I'm new to the area,' he said, 'and I can't speak about this man. So maybe one of the family would like to say a word on his behalf?'

Silence.

'Well, if the family are too upset, perhaps a friend could say a kind word?'

Silence.

'Surely there must be someone here who can say something good about this man.'

Slowly a man rose to his feet, pondered a few seconds and said, 'Well – his brother was worse.'

Gags over, an early night was demanded by tomorrow's schedule, so we crashed out and prepared for a good day. Did I say good? It was great! The four-ball was John, Chris, me and a lovely lady called Tracey Hammond. Tracey had been off the circuit for a while through illness, but what a comeback she made that day! Never missed a green.

La Princessa is a magnificent course – not easy

but then every golfer loves a challenge. I enjoyed the game and played reasonably well, delighting in a near miss for a hole in one, and completing nine holes with the same ball. During the round I met a charming man named David Phisick – 70-plus, full of wise sayings, good tales and cryptic dismissals of the various golf aids and gadgets when we tried them out on the practice ground.

'They'd never have allowed that in my day.'

'Waste of money.'

'Absolute tosh.'

(These, you understand, were his more complimentary remarks.)

All in all, a perfect day for golf, company and filming – plenty in the can, but never enough. Like golfers, film directors are never satisfied. I once witnessed a young pro shoot 64 gross at Royal Ascot on Tuesday, follow it with 66 on Wednesday and nearly sell his clubs in despair at the loss of form. I've often heard TV people say, 'That's absolutely perfect Tom. Let's just do it four more times for safety.' Talk about belt and braces!

Our ideal golf day must be perfect in every way. Of course, some people are never satisfied. You will recall the story of the dog carrying a basket that walked into the butcher's shop, put down the basket, yapped and nodded to a note in its collar. The amazed butcher made up the order and placed it in the basket. Then the dog opened its mouth, revealing teeth clenching a £20 note. The butcher took the note and put the change in the basket. The dog trotted out, followed by the butcher, who saw it stop at the pedestrian crossing, press the button, wait for the little green man to appear and toddle across the road. He followed the dog to a terraced house, where it unlatched the gate, bounced up to the door and pressed the bell. The door swung open and a rough-faced man grabbed the basket, snarled, and kicked the dog up the backside. Outraged, the butcher shouted out, 'How can you be so ungrateful to such a talented animal?'

'Talented, pal? Rubbish – that's three times this week he's forgotten his key!'

You see, we must know when to be satisfied.

OK – we have the ingredients for the ideal golf day: weather, wit, course. So now let's think of the characters who would be there to share the day.

7

Send for the 'A' Team

I WAS lucky to marry a Yorkshire lass, and I spent a lot of time in that fair county during my courting days. Being young and sharper than I am now, I soon realized that whenever four or more tykes are gathered round a pub table their first priority is to select an English cricket team from the greatest post-war players.

Naturally, the selection is utterly objective and untainted by county bias. In the case of my in-laws, the team would open with Hutton and Boycott. Truman and Illingworth would be bowling, Brian Close would be at number six, and they would certainly include Willy Watson, Johnny Wardle and exile Jim Laker. Of course, they would want to make room for Truman's oppo, Brian Statham, and they probably could not avoid including some effete southerners like Colin Cowdrey or Peter May. But the backbone of the side would, of course, come from Yorkshire.

Choosing a small, elite group from any facet of life is always fraught with danger and doubt, so I apologize up front for the next few pages, in which I indulge my privilege of choosing the people who would be present on my ideal golf day. They are not all golfers, but I will try to explain why I would want them there. Obviously people will disagree with some or all of the choices so, by way of being prepared, I recommend you have a pencil and paper nearby to list your arguments!

My golfing cadre comes from many walks of life. Real, fictional and apocryphal. Let's begin with the last category and highlight one of my all time heroes. The scene is a golf club party on the night of the captain's dinner. Festivities are at their height, disco blaring in the function room, old stories being renewed in the spikes bar, and serious revelry the order of the night.

Out into the car park stumbles a reveller, dropping his car keys on the ground and scrambling on hands and knees in the dark to retrieve them. Shuffling around aimlessly he finally recognizes his car and goes through the long laborious process of trying to get his key in the door lock. There's a lovely bit of visual business which I find hard to describe. It involves holding the loose end of your tie to the lock and sliding the key down the tie until it makes contact. Eventually, he finds his way into the car, humming a high-decibel version of 'Feelings'.

At the speed of light he then scorches around the car park leaving rubber in all parts, before driving out into the road, weaving just a little. Out of the gloom comes the police car that has been keeping the club under surveillance. It follows the reveller for about a minute, during which time his driving is strangely immaculate. Eventually, the policemen signal him to pull over and motion him out of the car. The following dialogue ensues.

> 'Now, sir, been to the golf club, have we?'
> 'That's correct, officer.'
> 'Been drinking, have we?'
> 'No officer, I'm teetotal.'
> 'Teetotal?'
> 'Can't stand the stuff – honestly.'
> Ten minutes and a negative breathalyser reading later, the frustrated policemen question our man further.
> 'Name?'
> 'Jim Watson.'
> 'Occupation?'
> 'Professional decoy!'

He would certainly be present on my golf day, even though he's only a legend. His is a good story, but it will always be a joke. Fact, as I will try to show, can be even funnier than fiction. Fact involving golfers can be funnier than anything else. Let me give you an example.

One of the trickiest audiences a comic can face is a ladies' hen night. Two or three hundred females, a running bar and devil take the hindmost. I was booked to appear at one such bash at a London hotel and found that on the bill was a very fine musical act, four-handed and veterans of much TV and radio exposure. Their road manager was planning the best place for the group to appear on the bill. Meanwhile, I was calling upon all my experience of crowds, heavily into drink, to do the same thing on my own behalf.

'We've decided we'd like to close the show,' said the roadie.

'All right by me,' says I, having realized that the ladies were going to be ever more difficult to please as the 'do' went on.

'Oh,' said the roadie, taken slightly aback. 'And we'd like to do our full time, 48 minutes!'

'That only leaves me 12 minutes,' I said, trying to look downcast, 'but I don't mind.' In fact, I was delighted.

To the admiration of the group and their minder I went on first and struggled to fill 12 minutes with enough material to keep the girls quiet. As I exited, almost to the sound of my own feet, the musical act were announced and they entered to their play-on. The music wasn't 'The Stripper' but it sounded like it, and that was enough for one of the more inebriated lasses. In a flash she was on a table top, kicking glasses everywhere and discarding all her clothing. She was down to her smalls before Security saved further blushes.

Next evening I was in a bar at Royal Ascot golf club telling our current captain, Alan Brabiner, the tale of the stripper.

'Don't tell me,' said Alan, 'the lady was five feet four, blue eyes, blonde hair, big boobs and beautiful legs.'

'No,' I said.

'They never are, mate. They never are!!'

Alan, that positive thinking earns you a place on the big day.

Speaking of Royal Ascot, I would have to include the members of my home club in my gallery for the ideal golf bash. My thanks to all of them, male and female, for being so kind to me over the years and particularly for allowing me to try out new gags on

'Sit down, Mother. It's not "The Stripper" anyway!'

them. I've been a member there for about 11 years and still enjoy the course. Shortish but tricky, it's never going to be taken apart by golfers good or even great. It's home to some wonderful characters, for instance Freddie Charlton, no longer a chicken but still a great player off his handicap. Straight down the middle and deadly on the greens. Freddie is the perfect partner in a competition, full of confidence and good advice – and the odd story, too.

Each character on my list will have his or her own story to be told. Take Tommy Cooper. Oh, how we miss him today! A man who could make people cry with laughter by doing absolutely nothing. If you ever saw his live act you'll know that for the first five minutes he wasn't even on stage. He used to pretend he was locked in the dressing room. Hysterics greeted his out of sight mutterings and mumblings. Even when he came on his act was totally off the wall.

'I jumped in a taxi the other day. I said "King Arthur's Close." '

The driver said, 'Don't worry, I'll lose him at the next set of lights.'

Tommy, a rib-tickling genius, was a dedicated golfer and caused uproar and mayhem on many a course and in many a clubhouse. A man of apparently ungovernable clumsiness, he was in fact capable of gliding like an ice skater when he moved. A total contradiction in terms but a legend for all time. We would need Tommy to set the tempo of the day – light hearted, carefree and relaxing. Tommy would cheer us, but who could organize us?

I'll give you my personal list of contenders and then tell you why they qualify. Argue if you wish, but you won't shake my conviction. My prime trio would be, in no particular order. Sir Billy Butlin, Kevin Keegan and Jimmy Tarbuck. An unusual combination I grant you, but each one an expert in his own sphere and an avid golfer, as well as devoting much time and effort to worthy charitable organizations.

Let's begin with a gentleman whom I never had the pleasure of meeting, the late Sir Billy Butlin, a man whose name lives on in the holiday centre complexes that he masterminded so many years ago. If ever a person was gifted with foresight it was Sir Billy. It's easy now to see how much the British public love being organized and entertained on a mass scale. But in the days after World War Two, with rationing, shortages and fun hard to find, it took a genius to predict what people would want in the way of leisure. Even now, in the 1990s, his family-style holidays provide the only real long-running summer season for hundreds of entertainers and variety shows, so showbiz as well as Joe Public has much to thank him for.

One of the classic stories about Butlin illustrates his astonishing attention to detail. Even in the very early days of holiday camps and family holidays, Billy had decided to give his centres a little style. So at the first of his venues, Filey, he made a point of highlighting the reception area in order to make a good and lasting impression on the new arrivals. The centrepiece was a huge goldfish pond – too big to be called a pool – inhabited by several hundred fish.

The great man would on occasion check in with a new wave of holidaymakers under an assumed name, and spend hours chatting to people, checking out the good points and possible failings in the system. How was the chalet? How good was the cabaret? What about the food? He would sneak around to the rear of the kitchens, checking the waste bins to see what was thrown away. Why are all those sausages going to waste? What's wrong with the fish cakes? And so on.

It was on one of these forays that Billy took off a bin lid and found a dead goldfish! Next morning he left the camp, returning a few hours later in his limo, having resumed the mantle of the Big Chief. After chatting with the management team about various topics, he led them across the reception area, then paused for a moment to stare at the pond.

'There's a fish missing!' he snapped.

'Y-y-yes, sir. I-I-It died last night,' spluttered the manager.

'If you died last night, would you have been replaced?' asked Billy.

'Yes, sir.'

'Well, put another fish in the pond!'

You can imagine the thoughts of the management team: 'My God, he even knows how many fish there are!!'

This is a man we must have in the clubhouse before and after the round. What stories he could tell!

So we have an entrepreneur and master organizer on our team. Now let's move onto the sportsman. I always maintain, often to the point of boredom, that golf is one of the last bastions of true sportsmanship. This is not to knock all the other sports or sportsmen, and one of my sporting heroes is ex-soccer star

'Coming sir, replacement's on its way sir!'

Kevin Keegan – a true Corinthian and a shining example to his fellow players and now one of the best young club managers in Britain. I once had the privilege to speak on Kevin's behalf in a TV soccer debate called 'Who's the Greatest?' and I'm delighted to say that we won.

The thing that strikes you first about Kevin is his infectious enthusiasm. But this is grounded in a deep awareness of the keys to success: practice, practice and practice again; listen to good advice, learn good habits and follow them; be mentally aware of what you can't do and don't attempt it. It all appears so simple when demonstrated by someone who is not only superbly gifted in ball games but possesses a razor-sharp mind. But we mere mortals should not despair – we must learn what we can from observing the legend. Kevin is a single-figure handicapper who could probably have been a pro had he not been so preoccupied by winning virtually every prize in soccer. Here is a man who can teach us much if we only bother to be bothered.

Devotion to golf we all have, else why carry on playing the game? Eagerness to improve we surely have, else why do we change clubs, balls, grip, swing at the slightest indication that they may provide 'the answer' at long last. Perseverance we have – or do we? Do we really have the right mental attitude for this game? Do we know what we want from it? Do we really understand the source of our obsession and the burning desire?

We can learn from a man like Kevin Keegan what it is that makes us come back day after day – generally for more punishment. Is it the feeling of triumph in victory? Is it the satisfaction of playing a good steady game and not duffing any shots – the hope of achieving the ultimate golfing goal, consistency? Nobody is so lucky that they escape from every bunker. Forget the twenty footer, nobody holes every two and a half foot putt unless he's practised the stroke, mastered the 'yips', learned to read the green, or learned to trust the word of a caddy who can.

Surely the most satisfying feeling in our golfing lives, fellow hacker, is lounging in the clubhouse and replaying a round where most balls went where aimed, most putts dropped or stopped near enough for a gimmie, the bag never felt lighter and the step was never so sprightly. We feel mentally invigorated, of course – in fact, we're more than ever likely to bore the pants off other members by repeatedly describing in excruciating, if poetic, detail that wonderful birdie we conjured out of the long par 4. But we also feel physically much less tired than usual because we've had to waste far less energy than usual in correcting errors that are inclined to plague our swing, stance, grip and so on. But whichever way you cut it, the chances of our playing well can only be enhanced by practice, the lack of a fuzzed-up head, the knowledge of what you can't do and the example of a real professional sportsman. Yes, Kevin would have to be in the team. He plays a very good game, is a gentleman to the core – and yes, he can tell a good tale.

It's not just for the tale-telling that our third organizer is Jimmy Tarbuck.

When a person is honoured by the half-hour programme *This Is Your Life* they know they have made it. When a full hour is dedicated to one person, he's got to be pretty extraordinary to deserve it. They've not only been there – they've been there and back. So it is with Tarby, who's been my personal idol since the first days he compered *Sunday Night at the London Palladium*. It could not have been easy for a 22-year-old up-and-coming comic, however full of cheeky patter and self-confidence. It would not have been easy for any comic of any age. It meant, above all, pressure, pressure and more pressure. Knowing what to do in the event of calamity and convincing everyone that you could be trusted to handle it. Having the right word to say at any given time. Tarby has always been ready to jump into a car and travel any distance to make up a golf team, or help a charity, or just be there. He's a man who gives his word and never goes back on it. And, most importantly, he's totally in love with golf, taking delight in any game in any company.

Tarby's infatuation with the game is so great it's almost tangible. His knowledge of golf is encyclopedic, and a handicap of six makes him both a fine golfer and a hard one to beat! We must have Jimmy on the big day – a countervailing force to the 'vocals' of Lee Trevino! Oh yes, Trevino would be there! So would a lot of great pros. If daylight were never-ending, we could include every golfer who played the great game. For now, let me just suggest a few personal favourites.

Peter Allis for sure would find a place. Here we have a man who not only played successfully at the highest level but almost single handedly (or voicedly) converted the Great British Public to enjoyment of armchair golf. How sweet the voice, how knowledgeable the words – he's numero uno among commentators. To my mind the luckiest bloke I know: still a very fine player, loves the sport, travels to beautiful places – and gets paid for it as well! We'd have to have Peter. And Seve, and Woosie and Faldo and that fine young player Colin Montgomerie. What a powerful hitter of a ball and what a gentle gentleman: it was a real treat to partner him in the Dunhill Masters. (If I could only putt, Colin, we might have won some glassware!)

Before my list becomes impossible to accommodate, let me mention a couple of guests who would be automatic choices of most golfing readers. Tony Jacklin must be there. One of the best strikers of a ball I've ever seen (or heard!). A winner both here and 'across the pond', he won the U.S. Open – by the ridiculous margin of seven shots – exactly half a century after the last Brit to do so. To date, none of the current crop of European greats – Seve, Faldo, Langer, Woosie – nor Greg Norman has managed to lay hands on that precious trophy. Jacklin was also, of course, the hugely inspirational captain of the European Ryder Cup team, the man who gave Europeans the confidence and belief in themselves not only to beat America, but to *expect* to beat them! Tony would be in my party, and maybe he'd bring along Nicklaus, Watson, Palmer, Crenshaw, Ray Floyd, Player and all those other wonderful names that light up the record books.

What tales they could tell – it would take a week of Wednesdays to hear them all. And how would we get them to talk? Easy – send for Parky. Michael Parkinson, for my money the finest TV interviewer here or elsewhere on sporting topics and (he'll tell you!) a very good golfer. He would get the best out of every star, comment on all facets of the game and be invaluable in all things except perhaps selecting a generally acceptable post-war English cricket XI, bearing in mind his Yorkshire origins.

'Hold up! – where are the ladies?' I hear you cry. Relax, I've not forgotten them. Let's start with Parky's missus – yes, Mary, TV presenter extraordinaire and possessor of a unique golf swing. According to no less a judge than Lee Trevino, not only is Mary's swing beautiful, she is the only player he's ever seen whose practice swing is exactly the same as the real one. Praise indeed. Mary would lead the ladies, along with Rachael Heyhoe Flint and my good pal Mia Carla – hilarious comic, bouncy personality and a good, and ever-improving, golfer. (Having been bountifully endowed bust-wise, Mia has adapted physically to golf by employing woods where possible instead of long and medium irons – I believe she even has a 9-wood in her bag – the longer shafts of woods compared to the irons enabling her to develop a more horizontal swing.)

Yes, golf's like that. Find what suits you and settle for that. Every game of golf should be like an extra birthday – look forward to it, play it, and then remember what you've got from it. Many things help to make my day when I play. Leaving plenty of time to get to the course, plenty of time to play the round (nothing worse than watching the time on every fairway and rushing through shots), and getting the most out of the company you play with.

On that subject, may I suggest that on our special day we would also have the company of the legendary Frank Carson – but wearing a muzzle. It is said that Harley Street took a sample of Frank's saliva and used it as a cure for lockjaw. In fact, a quiet Carson is a dangerous man – he's generally putting together a winning score. With him we'd never be short of a gag, on or off the course, in the bar, on the bus home or up your lobby if you let him follow you. Bless you, Frank, you're a one off.

My list of names is growing by the minute and is far from complete. But I think it's time to pause – reassess the characters yet to be included and look at the situation so far. We know who and what we need on our ideal day. We know the weather and the location we would have. But what about the individual holes we are to play – where would they come from? Well, like the company, from everywhere. Lend an ear while I tell you.

8

If My Uncle Had Been a Woman He'd Have Been My Auntie!

THERE ARE so many conversations in life that include the line 'if only'. In golf, every conversation includes it! Oh, if only we could replay a round, or a particular hole, or just a bunker shot – and how that would have made a difference. Probably our own situation would not be as earth-shatteringly altered as, say, would be a mistake in the Ryder Cup or the Open (remember Hale Irwin's air shot over a one-inch putt?) Nevertheless there is room in our reverie to go once again over familiar and much-loved battlefields and replay the shots with the perfect swing of hindsight. My usual wont is to cover just one particular course and remember the best scores on each hole – usually I end up about 12 under par with an eclectic card. This time, though, I'm taking the holes from everywhere, home and abroad, more with the intention of recalling a story or tip that might help the reader, and always with the intention of looking on the brighter side.

The holes come in no particular order but only as they spring to mind. However, the first *is* a first hole: number one on the West course at Wentworth, the Burma Road. Surely this is one of the most daunting opening holes in golf.

A yard or two short of a par 5, at 471 yards it is a very tough par 4. You tee off over a road which is in constant use and you require a carry that seems endless. It's a real test of bottle. This is emphatically not a situation where you arrive late, change shoes in the car park, and sprint without loosening up to the tee, have a wafty practice swing and then launch yourself at the ball. No, it's time for relaxed preparation. After all, there are all those people watching in the car park, on the putting green, in the pro shop, in the clubhouse, on the road. My God, this is an impossible hole – and I haven't even addressed the ball yet! No, hold on, keep calm, admit what you can't do, admit that your chances of hitting the green in two are in the realms of the miraculous. Why not, as the wise man once said, pretend the hole is a par 5 and try to birdie it. Now that makes it all seem easier, doesn't it? Nobody expects you to boom two woods to within a foot or so of the pin and drop the putt. Be satisfied with a five, and jump up and down if you get a four.

This hole taught me two lessons in one, and I've never forgotten either. Never be daunted by the length of carry or the yardage. Play a steady down the middle game, because a ball in play for three is much better than a ball in the trees for two. Why try to smash the guts out of the ball to no avail? For this reason, I hardly ever carry a driver in my bag. Even if I say to myself, I hit a goodish length with a 3-wood and generally keep it straight with just a hint of a draw. My game remains enjoyably steady while it is in my hand – but change to a driver, the big timber, and suddenly everything falls apart. The swing shortens, the downswing accelerates too soon, breathing deepens and blood pressure goes through the roof! OK, once in a while I hit a screamer, but never more than 15 yards further than my normal 3-wood – so what's the point? In any case, extra distance on some holes means more complications in selecting clubs for the second shot. So leave the big hitting to the pros, treat long par 4s as par 5s and remember the first at Wentworth with affection, not trepidation.

After a tricky long hole let's take a tricky short one. Surely there's nothing more infuriating than having the ammunition to reach a green but never actually achieving it. So as our second, let's play the second on the Duke's course at Woburn golf club, as played in the Dunhill Masters Pro-Celebrity-Am. A beautiful picturesque hole in any weather: tee on a woody hill top, the green at the bottom of the steep hill, little more than 130 yards away but guarded by two bunkers on each side. (I think it's hole three on the normal card.)

I've played it five times over the Dunhill years and never been nearer to the pin than 20 feet. I've used everything from a sand wedge to a 6-iron depending on conditions and still get the wobbles in club selection even though the scene is so serene. There's usually a huge gallery sitting on the grass, probably one of the most knowledgeable crowds in golf, and, boy, am I ever glad that it's a Texas Scramble so it's not disastrous for my team if I fail here. A good second hole for our day.

One long, one short, both tricky. So what about

an easier one for our third? Remember we have the power to alter things to suit our own wants and needs. So excuse me if I choose the sixteenth on my home course of Royal Ascot. It's not quite as easy as it looks: 280 plus yards tee to green, but lots of bother between (that could be a line from a song!). A good 7-iron shot from the tee lies a concrete ditch running right across the fairway. To the right and reachable with a long 5-iron is out of bounds on the cricket pitch, while to the left, with even less club, you can be out of bounds in the reservoir. Yes, there is fairway but not a lot of it. The green can be driven on a good day with the wind in your favour, but the way my pal John O'Neill and I play it is much simpler. Par 4 means on the green for two and two putts, so why not two 8 or 9-irons, depending on the wind, and maybe a putt for birdie. No hassle, no heartache, no lost ball. A very satisfying third hole.

Would you mind if I stayed near home for the next one? It's just that when I've played it I can pop over to our house for a mug of tea or something stronger. I live in Swinley Forest, you see, and from that lovely course with its beautiful lawn-like fairways let me choose the eighteenth. For this hole I'd be in the company of Ian Pearce, club secretary and two handicapper, Bob the professional, and possibly Les, five handicapper and steward of the club. A raised tee and nothing more to carry than a ditch about 150 yards away, the hole is nevertheless fraught with danger. Out of bounds and thick trees to the left all the way down. On the right are wide expanses which lead to the first fairway, but young trees on this side are gradually beginning to come into play. For me the greatest hazard lies in the choice of club for the approach shot. A good drive and you're looking up at the green behind which, in quick succession are a service road, the putting green, the patio, and the clubhouse, wall clock and all. Here lies the title of this particular book. On my first ever foray down this fairway, and standing behind a well-driven ball, I was advised by a regular to use a 4-iron to the green. Never stopping to check yardage I smashed the ball over the clubhouse and into the car park at the rear, en route scattering practice-putters, after-lunch drinkers, and asphalters in the back yard. Now, though, it's one of my favourites – touch wood – and since that slight case of overkill I've never had worse than a par 4 and managed a few birdies on the way. So that's hole number 4, and now it's into the clubhouse to have a word with Pat about how the day is going.

Suitably refreshed, let's go international – well, to Scotland anyway and one of my favourite courses north of the border – Nairn. It was while entertaining in pantomime in the mid-1980s that I first played this fine championship course, one of a string of jewels 'twixt Royal Aberdeen and magnificent Royal Dornoch. I've rarely met such hospitality from club members and staff, and it was here that I hit my best ever drive – the one that brings me back to try again, the one that still messes with my emotions.

We've all heard fantasies of the world's longest drive – half a mile on a frozen lake – seven leagues on the moon, where there's no wind resistance. My favourite is the one hit onto a moving train in Wigan and ending up in Truro, Cornwall – having changed at Crewe, of course!

'You're going the wrong way clever Dick. The Truro train goes from platform two!'

But we're looking at the serious stuff at Nairn, the superlative seventh hole – around 500 yards all along the edge of the Moray Firth and no margin of error on the right. I was playing with a local chap, Alan, whose complete game would make him a sure money-winner if he were to turn pro. He could hit the ball a country mile with pinpoint accuracy, and the tempo of his swing was something to watch and emulate, if only I could! I had just bought a one-off hybrid driver for £30 (those were the days!). Ryder head, Prosimmon shaft, Mizuno grip – beautifully weighted and handsome to behold.

Under Alan's instructions I had used a 3-wood for the opening holes to groove in my swing. But on the seventh I let go with the driver and can honestly say that a ball never left the screws quite like it: almost 300 yards, given a generous, bone-hard fairway to bounce on. My steady 5-wood finished on the green, and my longish eagle putt lipped the hole. So I just had a tap in for a birdie four that still makes the memory tingle. Yes, this would be my fifth hole – it's the reason I am still tempted to keep a driver in my bag.

On to the sixth and where to next? Somewhere in the Emerald Isle, I think – hey, what about the first at Portmarnock? Yes, that's a good one for all the right reasons. It's Ireland's premier tournament course, it's a links course handy for Dublin's airport and it's where I first met the legendary Harry Bradshaw, who was for many years the professional there. The first is quite a straightforward par 4, just shy of 390 yards: little bother with your tee shot, but take care your mid-iron approach avoids the bunker guarding the front left of the green. The reason it is so special is the feeling of total calm and well-being that the surroundings imbue on one of those lovely soft, sunny Irish mornings. Sure, the world has gone away and for a little while there's nothing else in life but this tee, that fairway and yonder green. The fact that I've never done worse than par the hole owes all to the ambience, and this I would need after the great temptation to use my driver on the previous hole. So Portmarnock for the sixth. Then it's northward for the seventh.

There are certain mystical, magical courses which I seem destined never to play: Dornoch, which was too far to reach even when I was in panto in Inverness; Gleneagles, where three times I was beaten by the weather; and Royal Portrush although I did make a start there.

Having agreed to a tour of Ulster I was treated right royally by one and all and invited to play everywhere I went. I enjoyed every course, but remember mostly the four-ball at Portrush. We met on a blustery, wind-swept day when the rain hit your face like bullets and the brain went numb at the thought of four hours of purgatory ahead. My caddy, Seamus, a man mentioned in dispatches in *From the Wood to the Tees*, was as chipper as possible in the conditions and talked me through the par 4 first, where I holed a long putt by 'ignoring the swing and belting it through the spray'. On to our featured hole the par 5-second – 497 yards and slight dogleg left: quite straightforward, you might think – but that takes no account of the elements. Boy, I've never been so cold, so wet, so miserable, so in need of a large brandy. Yet those 497 yards contained three spectacular shots: each time, the club slipped

out of my hands – on two occasions the club travelling further than the ball. I think my score was
11 and the green just about within range of another
club-throw when I picked up and delightedly agreed
with my partners that the clubhouse was the place
for lost souls such as we. Perhaps luckily, we aban-
doned the round before we had tackled two of
Portrush's trickiest holes, the aptly named Purgatory and Calamity Corner, the latter one of the
greatest short holes in Europe.

Out of the gales and into the sun. For our eighth,
how about the 18th at Acapulco's Princess course.
It features a carry of 120 yards of water from the
tee, just one tree, then a nice wide fairway with few
hazards leading to a beautifully manicured green.
If you recall my previous book, it was here that our
entire four-ball ended in the water (we had, as the
saying goes, 'drink taken', not realizing that the gin
in these parts is 150 proof and rising). Still and all,
this is a finishing hole that sees the warm sun on
your back and there is a delightful awareness that
you're on a relaxing holiday and that, even if you
make an absolute porridge of the hole you can
come back tomorrow to put it right – or, indeed, a
completely different porridge. So it's Acapulco two
before the turn, and then back to Blighty: back to
my old stomping ground of Merseyside.

Time for another par 3 to finish the half, so why
not pick one on a course that has a special history
all its own. Home of many great tournaments, many
moments of triumph and tragedy, it's a course that
used almost to be in my own back yard: Royal
Birkdale, no less. I moved there from Formby in
1976. You'll recall that Johnny Miller won the Open

at Birkdale that year, while in joint second place –
playing in his first Open – was 19-year-old Seve
Ballesteros. The sun never stopped shining that
summer: all was terribly well with the world, and I
was appearing in Blackpool.

It was the first time I had topped a theatre bill,
and I learnt so very much about show business from
that brilliant act, Ronnie Dukes and Ricky Lee
('This place reminds me of home – filthy dirty and
full of strangers').

The late Ronnie was a good golfer and a man I
partnered many times – but not on this particular
day at Birkdale. My team included members of the
'youth club' (over 70s) and Stan Roderick, brother
of the old champion boxer Ernie. Stan it was at the
par 3 seventh who recommended I use a 7-iron. I
was sure it was too much for the 150-odd yards
down-wind, but I did what we must all do in the
circumstances: stay with the club you've chosen and
give it the treatment. As previously recorded my
shot cleared the green and was making a fair bid to
reach the eighth fairway when Stan chose to add a
rider to his club selection:

'Not *that* hard!'

But nothing daunted, I chipped back on to the
green and holed out for my first-ever par on a
championship course. So this I remember when we
include Birkdale in our front nine.

Guess what? We've reached the half-way so it's
time for a welcome break for a jar, a bun and a
chance to compare notes. We'd surely have a huge
marquee, a free bar, sausage sandwiches – and
sound-proofing in case Frank Carson's within a mile
and playing badly!

9

'I Lost Five Pounds Yesterday.'
'Strict Diet?'
'No, Count-back on the Second 9.'

WE'RE ONTO the 10th and for some reason actual
10th holes feature strongly in my list of 18. But let's
start back with one of the more famous 10ths – that
on the Brabazon course at The Belfry. Seve's hole,
as legend has it. Who can forget that super drive of
almost 280 yards hit with perfectly calculated fade
so that it cleared the water and settled neatly on
the green. Oh, that we mere mortals could just *once*
hit a shot like that! Still, we can dream!

I've become almost the resident comedian at The
Belfry over the years. Golf days, corporate con-
ferences, after-dinner speeches, presentations – it
seems I'm hardly ever away from the place. Pat and
I have been privileged to watch it grow into the
excellent sporting centre it is today, its facilities
unmatched by anywhere else I've been to. Wouldn't
it be nice to describe how well I've played there?
Trouble is, there are too many witnesses. I've had
so many traumas on the 10th it not only sickens me,
it almost hurts to hear people say: 'One down the
left, two onto the green, three in the hole: three,

nett two – four points.' Doesn't anybody have my record of inconsistency? Not once a par, only twice a bogey. The 10th is my permanent card wrecker – despite the finest advice at hand.

My first brush with this beast was while guesting at the finals of the BMW Classic. Booked as after-dinner speaker and bon viveur, I was overjoyed to be asked to play with the boss of BMW and that great professional and tutor, John Jacobs. What a giant of a man he is, in all respects; a man whose expertise can straighten any swing and change any outlook for the better. With never a negative thought in his head, he is an object lesson in how to learn from every shot and every situation.

I remember a brief exchange as we passed each other at Glasgow airport:

'All right, John, I'm keeping my head down and swinging slow.'

'It's head up son, but don't tell anyone – it keeps me in work!'

Now, was he joking? I daren't ask!

Back to the BMW Classic and, after a reasonably good card on the outward nine, sound advice from the master: 'Take a 5-iron down the left towards the tree, sand wedge to the green, and who knows? Three putts for a net par or even better, maybe.'

I hit the perfect 5-iron as instructed and marched spring-heeled towards the ball, full of those positive thoughts enjoined by the sports psychologists. With sand wedge in hand, I threw a few blades of grass into the air (it makes no sense to me, but it looks good) and selected the point on the green where I was going to put the ball. Practice swing. Nice and relaxed at address. A good, slow swing and my ball soars up and falls in a graceful arc into the centre of the pond. Hell's teeth – not *again*!

'What did you get there, Tom?'

'Just a blob, John. Just a blob!'

But don't fall into the error of thinking that's my only route to disaster on this hole. Earlier this year I hit the statutory mid-iron down the left, pitched nicely onto the green, and *putted* into the water, for heaven's sake! So it's not my favourite hole, but one that is unforgettable. So my 10th is the 10th at The Belfry.

Without letting the Irish in me take over, the 11th is another 10th – well, you know what I mean. It's the 10th on the card at Childwall, Liverpool. Childwall is a smashing club, with a delightful body of members, and it's never short of volunteers when charity days loom. Here it was that I met my pals Jimmy Mac ('give them nothing!') and Douggie. If there is such a thing as a laugh a hole these two giants of the construction industry provide it. They're two who've been there and back, and made the most of the journey. What particularly impresses me about their golf is that they can play as well or as badly as you – but they always seem to manage to take the money! Many's a cold autumn morning we've struggled around the front nine waiting for the swing to groove itself in, or pigs to fly, or lightning to strike. And then we come to the 10th. It's a great par 5 almost reachable in two on a good day (with a following gale and a 100 yard bounce).

Twice, memorably, I've reached the edge of the green, then chipped and one-putted and changed the entire course of the game (not to mention the tone of their language). But my magical moment

'Eh up! Better take cover,
O'Connor's about!'

occurred when, unknown to us, a family of gypsies had encamped over the fence to the right of the fairway. Two boomers (3-wood, 5-wood) and I'm just short of the dance floor. Then, as if by magic, a blur of a figure came flying from the fence area, picked up the ball and was gone again. Jim and Douggie claimed they had been admiring the interesting cloud formations and hadn't seen a thing. But after lengthy negotiations to which I should have brought my solicitor and accountant, they allowed me to place another ball and carry on. In return for this kindness, I was to allow them a few 20-foot gimmies on the greens. For weeks afterwards I played that hole with a spotter near the green, until Jim and Douggie explained that the gypsies had moved away the very next morning! Still, a happy 11th.

For my 12th I choose yet another 10th – a really testing par 4 at Torquay golf club, one of the friendliest clubs I've ever visited. It's 13 years since my first visit – and how the memories came flooding back! I was in my third season as top of the bill for Bernard Delfont and appearing at the Festival Theatre in Paignton. As usual I was looking around for somewhere to play for the summer. Stage manager Derek Smith arranged temporary membership at Torquay, and there I played virtually every day throughout the season. A good course, fine weather, plenty of partners and the happiest 12 weeks were about to unfold.

Alan Egford was the professional (see my story about him in *From the Wood to the Tees*) and he taught me much both on and off the course. We organized several charity Celebrity-Ams and I was amazed to find how willing the members were to help. Nothing was too much trouble and not even the switching of times, days and even club seating arrangements flustered the good folk of Torquay. Michael, the club steward (originally from Poland I think), had a beaming smile and lovely personality which seemed to brighten every corner of the clubhouse. The meals were great and the beer was just right.

Here I broke 80 for the first time, and here I finally got my handicap down to single figures. Here I even won an inter-celebrity competition to the chagrin of The Bachelors, The Wurzels and several other stars who demanded an immediate cut in my handicap, or a public enquiry, or both. I attributed it to the weather. You see, because of differing start and finish times of our various shows in the town, the competition was played to the very loosest of time scales – first light until 10.30 off the first tee. My partner, Dick Richardson, ex-European heavyweight boxing champion, and I went out at 7am in bright, breezeless conditions and had a very relaxing morning – no one in front and no one pressing behind.

At the turn I had a gross score of 39 and was very chuffed to say the least. Then came the 10th, a long par 4. You drive from an elevated tee, and there is plenty of trouble on the left – bad news for a draw-side player like me. There's plenty of room on the right, but don't stray too far or you will block out your second shot.

Dick had laid into one that seemed to climb forever and then bounce quite nicely right into the fluffy semi-rough. I had already decided to use a driver. Now, you know already that the driver and

I are incompatible. But, I thought, if this is going to be my day, let's make it in spades. (If disaster ensued, I could always keep just the front half of the score card.)

Boom! The driver went through my ball and hoisted it many a mile, down the middle with a slight draw. 'If you'd walked down the fairway and placed it you couldn't have put it in a better spot,' said Dick. 'Now don't make a pickle of the second!'

Powered equally by adrenalin and fear of upsetting this fine boxer, I proceeded to repeat the drive on a smaller scale, rifling a 5-wood straight and true, pin high and 10 feet to the right of the flag. Wow! Surely even I could par the hole from that distance? I tried to work out the line of my putt; it appeared one minute to be left to right, the next right to left. Then came the wisest words I've ever heard on a green. Dick said: 'Look, son, all putts are straight if you hit them hard enough!' Good thinking – well, positive thinking anyway.

Head down, no blinking, no fear, no thought of tomorrow, I hit the ball such a whack that it streaked straight at the hole, hit the back of the cup, flew about a foot in the air and dropped back in! A birdie! None of your mundane pars, pal – a birdie! I wanted to run to the clubhouse and tell everyone. Instead I wrote 3 on the card and vowed to keep my game together. And I did: a round of 78, half a dozen putts that hit the back of the hole and dropped. (Also, two putts that missed the back of the hole and finished further away than they started – you can't win 'em all.)

Meanwhile, the clouds were gathering, the wind began to howl, and the other competitors were blown to kingdom come – leaving Dick and me first and second. That day I saw grown men cry, clubs bent over knees, balls thrown away and whole golf sets up for sale. My fellow entertainers were unanimous in their generous praise of my performance – it's not easy to say 'well done' through clenched teeth. Altogether, I've never been so happy. What a good 12th hole!!

Time for another par 3 now, and time to switch from ecstasy to agony – or at least the strong possibility of it. It's also time to go back to my roots, Merseyside, and back in time to the glorious days of the 1970s. Everything seemed to go well for me that decade – endless summers, success on TV, and golf, golf, golf. We were living in Birkdale for most of this time and it became important to try and join a golf club. Funnily enough, and for various reasons, this wasn't possible; but the nearest I came to membership was at Southport & Ainsdale golf club, one of a succession of wonderful, championship-quality courses between Liverpool and Southport.

Having met the captain and generally put myself about the clubhouse, I played as often as possible in order to meet more and more members and hopefully persuade a couple to sponsor me. All this involved paying full-bat green fees for myself and whoever I could find to partner me. But it was well worth the effort. The S & A is a severe, if delightful, test of golf, wind or no wind, as plenty of Open qualifiers would tell you. To me it was a supreme achievement to play to my handicap there. In fact it was here that I first truly understood the significance of a conversation I had, at another club, with a Scotsman.

'What's your handicap?' he asked.

'Eight,' I said.

'Where?'

Yes, it is important that courses are taken into consideration when assessing a player's ability. Some courses are infinitely more difficult than others, irrespective of length. The S & A examines the credentials of every golfer – and it isn't made any easier if your partner is giving you duff advice! I had a choice of holes I could have picked from this fine course, each with its own related story. Take the 18th, a par 4 littered with humps and hollows, and blind shots. You need a guide dog and a compass. The first time I played it my partner instructed:

'Three-wood, just left of the marker.'

I duly hit a spoon, sweet as a nut if I may say so, and as it flew left of the stick, he sighed: 'Well, that's gone. Indian country – there's snakes in there.'

'I did what you said.'

'Yeah, but the wind dropped.' (I remember chasing him to the clubhouse, but I can't remember which club I hit him with.)

On one occasion I reached the green in two and saw my road-manager and partner Tommy rushing up to the crowd milling around, shouting, 'Look where the boss is for two!' Naturally, overawed by the gathering throng, I four-putted – just to give them their money's-worth, you understand.

When I mentioned possibly agonies at the S & A, I meant them to apply not to the 18th but to the first. I don't know about you, but I prefer a course to start with a shortish par 5, just gentle enough to let you settle into the game with little hassle. The first at Southport (as at Royal Lytham, across the Ribble estuary) is the exact opposite: a very cute par 3, well guarded and an extremely testing pipe-opener.

My only complaint about the hole is that a player can hit a fairly indifferent iron shot and make the green – and never know the problems he would have faced had he missed. Here is a hole which, if you par it, doesn't necessarily presage a satisfying round. On the other hand, if you miss the green you may be in card-wrecking country. Yes, this is a hole that requires respect, a proper warm-up and a silent prayer before teeing off. Luckily, we don't have to have it as the opener for our perfect day. No, its position would be 13 – unlucky for some.

OK, let's have a little fun now – or at least lighten the seriousness of the round. Let's bring back the memory of a good hole that made me smile with satisfaction, grimace with annoyance and laugh in surprise – not in that order but certainly all on the same day. I'm referring to the 9th at Royal Eastbourne.

Of all my summers away from home, I recall that of 1979 the most vividly. I was appearing at Eastbourne's Congress Theatre for the season and had gratefully accepted the offer of temporary membership of the golf club. There was no shortage of partners that summer – most of the band played golf, as well as several of the cast. Here it was that my good friend Dave Evans attempted to learn the game. Dave, a brilliant comedian, impressionist and musician, just didn't have the patience for golf. Apparently he tried even Val Doonican – Mr Cool himself – to the point of exasperation.

When my friend became too angry to play, I found a new friend in the club pro, Neil Large, an expatriate Scouser and a great teacher. Many's the nine holes we played, either half the main course or the nine-holer, or what they called 'the loop', which includes a bit of both. It was good to learn as I played – facing real situations and being shown how to deal with them. Here is where I saw Neil's assistant duff a drive and hurl the driver after the ball, walk up to the club – and throw it again! (Dammit, even that arch-hurler Tommy Bolt, U.S. Open champ of 1958, used to ration himself to one throw per shot.)

However, on the occasion I have in mind, the sun shone, the early morning coffee tasted as good as it smelled, and Neil and I had played a good opening eight holes and had teed off from the 9th, across the road and safely onto the fairway. Now came the first hint that it would be an unusual day. Walking up the fairway to our drives, we became aware that we were not alone. No, not extraterrestrials, not ghosts, but sunbathing holidaymakers who, driving along the road which separates the two halves of the course, had discovered what seemed the perfect spot to lie topless on freshly mown grass.

What to do? Isn't it odd that on occasions like that, though you have a perfect right to be there, you feel like an intruder? Should we shout, warning them of an approach? Should be walk past them with a cheerful 'Good morning!? Or should we do what any other golfer would do? Head down, play an iron to the green and pretend they weren't there? Yes, that's what we did and fortunately we got away with it. We felt somehow that we'd escaped the worst – but that was to come.

The 13th at Royal Eastbourne is a really good par

'Just look at those cheeky devils. Tell 'em to clear off, Trevor!'

3 with a downhill carry of about 170 yards all the way to the green. The hole has always been an enigma for me. A bad shot can bounce on and stay; a good one can hit the green, take off like a rocket and disappear for ever. Neil's drive (a 7-iron I think) landed almost stone dead, maybe two feet from the flag. I was already conceding the hole when a crow (the devil incarnate, said Neil) swooped down and, thinking his ball to be an egg or some desirable object, proceeded to knock it off the green in its efforts to pick it up. I sportingly stifled my howls of laughter (the players on the next fairway only pretended to be startled by the noise) and, agreeing that the rules of golf were disgracefully unfair, led the way to the 14th tee.

The 14th at Royal Eastbourne – and this is the 14th on our card as well – is a great par 4. It's a dogleg of more than 350 yards, the right bend being almost 90 degrees. On the right is trouble in the form of out of bounds and high trees. The safe shot in anyone's book is a long iron or 5-wood straight down the fairway and maybe a 5 or 6-iron to the green. Unfortunately, I was still in my golfing childhood, wanting to 'lamp' the ball as far as possible. So, flushed with Neil's recent embarrassment, I lined up over the high trees on the right, teed the ball a little higher than normal and smashed a 3-wood high and handsome over the corner and flush onto the fairway.

'I know another guy who played that shot,' said Neil, 'and he was an animal as well!'

I'd like to say I rounded off the hole with a par. But the problem with the long hit, as so often happens, is that it left me uncertain as to what to play to the green. Bump and run with an 8-iron, pitch with the wedge, a high sand iron, hoping it will stop? I chose the wedge, hit it too hard, and saw the ball bounce into the trees behind the green, never to be found. Still, we'll take the 14th at Eastbourne.

When first considering the venues of our ideal round, you'll recall the weather was important as well as the facilities and partners. Another vital ingredient emerges as we take our place on the 15th tee. That ingredient is the beauty of the setting. And if we make a literal interpretation of Walter Hagen's advice to smell the flowers on the way, what better place to be than the 17th on La Princessa at La Manga, already decided by me to be the host venue. This hole has one of the nicest fairways to stroll down while in the enjoyable process of completing a good card and having no cares about time or the elements. It's 479 metres long (my dad would say 'That's even longer in yards!' He's right, it's all of 524 yards), a dogleg left with water, and very ornately presented water, on the right. Here's a hole where much depends on a good drive: you want to keep as close to the *aqua* as possible without going in. No use being greedy for your second and trying to hammer a wood to the green for two. It's impossible for mere mortals such as we. No, keep to the safety of a long iron or small wood to land short, and leave a full short-iron shot to the pin.

I've played the hole only twice, once buggy-assisted (very nice) but once carrying the bag (albeit in the early evening away from the sun's glare) and having time to marvel at the vision, technical knowhow and hard work that must have gone into its creation. And to appreciate the non-stop care and attention it requires to maintain the beauty of what is a masterpiece of landscaping rather than a track to lose your temper on! When you come to think of it, that is true of most golf holes on the great courses world wide. We should perhaps take more time to soak up the beauty, the care, the design, the loving labours that these tracks have lavished upon them in plenty.

Yes, La Manga, you've done it again! You've got me dreamy-eyed and thinking of higher things than hacking at a ball. You've got me preaching the finer points of golf, the supreme essence of the supreme game. The game that unites all people of all classes, creeds, nationalities and occupations.

I once remarked to a grumbling partner, 'I know you're having a hard time, Geoff, but there's plenty of people in the cemetery who'd change places with you.'

'Not the way I'm playing,' said Geoff.

But we're all like that every now and again. Golf takes us by the throat just as much because we play badly as because, every now and again, we play well. In fact, our obsession with this game depends on the contrast between these ups and downs. All I can say is, if you're really down, get out on the 17th at La Manga: feel the sun on your back, wonder at the lawn-like fairway, the flowers, the water – and thank heaven you play golf!

Back to Britain now, and the 18th at Moor Park – for a lot of reasons. To begin with to pay tribute to a deservedly famous golf club. It's home to many a prestigious competition, including the Coca-Cola Classic. Here on two consecutive occasions I have been invited to play, and both times I was able to fit in photographic sessions for this book and the previous one (the picture on the dust jacket was taken on Moor Park's High Course). My thanks to Jim Couton, U.K. trading director of Coca-Cola, for the yearly invitation. It's nice to keep in touch with a fellow Liverpudlian whose father was one of my comedy heroes. Jim senior and his dog Rex were an integral part of my early days in showbusiness. I was a mere folk singer, but long admired the comedians' craft and no one represented it better than Jim. He was a fine talker, too, a master of the one liner:

New apprentice at Cammell Laird shipyard to foreman:

'Can I have a sub, guv?'

'Certainly, if you can get it through the gates!'

'What's the quickest way to the hospital, barman?'

'Drink that big fella's pint!'

Sadly missing you, Jim, but you'd be proud of your lad – he's done well!

Coca-Cola's big day is organized by another pal of mine, Nick Lunn, my early days coach at Ascot and now extremely successful in the promotions field. Naturally, with friends like these around me, I look forward to playing once a year, and you would think I'd play well. No way! I don't know why. Never once! Last year we played three balls, with an extra yellow ball. Do you know the set-up? Each player keeps his own score, but once every three holes he plays the yellow ball for the team score. Teams are allowed to lose two yellow balls before they're out of the race. This year, backed by my pal Peter Barnes, who was hitting woods for the first time, we lasted a grand total of two holes, scoring points on neither and coming last. Several others had no points but lasted more holes than we did. This form of golf is not recommended under any circumstances, but especially if you are playing with someone whose friendship you value.

But I digress. Let us return to our special day and the 18th on the High Course. It's 152 yards, or a little shorter off the front tee. You have to hit over a road which suddenly comes alive with traffic in the middle of your back swing, and it's not an easy green to find. It's well guarded by bunkers and there are trees on the right. Both years I've made the green and stayed on. On one occasion I won the 'nearest the pin' prize. I was presented with a super painting, a special-edition print. Of Moor Park? No, of Turnberry! Sometimes I think Jim Couton is trying to rival his father in the comedy stakes. Still, we have our 16th hole for the big day.

Let's give our course a four, three finish by taking the first at Gorleston golf club, near Great Yarmouth. Here it was that my golf career began, under the watchful eye of George Willard, golf pro, gentleman and one of the finest ambassadors of the sport it has been my pleasure to meet: meticulous when it comes to golf etiquette; relaxed and far-seeing when playing, and patient beyond the call of duty when teaching mugs like me.

'Remember the pendulum. Our old friend the circle. Pick the club up and swing *through* the ball. It's a golf *swing* not a golf hit.'

His words stay with me like a 'times table' learned long ago. I'm grateful to this lovely man who, I'm delighted to report, still turns out every Friday morning for a round. He'll still be playing the first the way he taught me. It's a par 4 of 258 yards, with bunkers left and right at 200 yards, and again on each side of the green.

'Let's remember that we'll need two clubs to reach the green,' he would say to me – he knew I wanted to smash a driver as hard as I could, but he restrained me. 'Our second,' he would continue, 'needs to be a full shot so that we can relax over the ball and hopefully place it near enough to the flag to hole in two putts.'

Gentle George, how right you were! O'Connor (1977 version) stood on the tee and hit a 7-iron down the middle, short of the fairway bunkers. Calmly O'Connor strode up and hit another 7-iron pin high, and then two putted for his first ever par! Good hole, good golf club, great pro. Thanks, George!

Homeward bound now. We've got to remember that after a long and tricky round of golf we'll need victuals and ale aplenty to recharge the batteries. So no apologies for the 18th. It's an 18th hole in its own right, the closing hole at Penwortham golf club, south of Preston.

Many a pleasant day I've spent on this wooded parkland course on the banks of the River Ribble. Secretary John Parkinson and I have battled many a day with the elements, the course and each other for serious money – notably the price of the delicious buttered scones. It's always a good day at Penwortham, but it's always a relief to reach the 18th green!

Cardiac Hill, as Tommy my manager calls it (yes, there's another such at Torquay), begins among trees and ends 178 yards later at a well-bunkered green outside the clubhouse. This makes the par 3 double difficult. Club selection is all, and could result in a crowd of chair-bound members ducking for cover, or a shot short of the green which will take much puffing and panting to reach, and hopefully chip on. It's a bit like trial by public enquiry while negotiating the North Face of the Eiger. So it's no surprise that people enter the clubhouse drained, puffed out and, sometimes, happy to still be alive.

But what the heck, on our ideal golf day we'll feel no pain or strain – and waiting indoors will be ex-steward Joe Kay and his good lady. They will prepare a mixed grill like no other. Half a cow, half a pig, two sheep, a dozen fried eggs, the contents of Walls' sausage factory, an entire bakery, and two or three local breweries to wash it down. Yes, that's where we'll sit and eat, and talk and grumble, and swap stories. John Parkinson, who has heard it all before, will greet us in his own, special way:

'You've obviously had a great day, I know you're dying to tell me all about it, and I can't wait to hear. But I've got a bit of a headache, so why don't you start at the 18th!'

Well, we've certainly got a tale to tell. A course made up of holes from everywhere. Par 71. Every green hit in regulation, every hole parred. No losers, no winners, no flukes, no disasters. No cheats, no back stabbers. This is what it's all about, this is why we bother. This, and just one or two other things.

10

'If I Were You, I'd Jack Up His Cap and Slide Another Player Underneath.'

WE'VE A fine 18-hole course to play and some fine company to enjoy on the Great Day – so what else do we need? Well, let's look at what we *don't* need first.

Although I insist that golf is the one true bastion of sportsmanship and fair play, you know and I know that cheating does exist. Even though the person involved is only cheating himself, and long-term it does him no good, we must not allow it to ruin our perfect day.

So we won't have the player who carries two balls in his pocket which have the same make and number as the one in play. He is the one whose ball is never lost, always finds his own ball in the rough, and who always has a clear shot out of trouble. His brother, not quite so evil but still unacceptable, is the one who goes up to his ball in the rough and, in spite of the fact that everyone knows it's his ball, insists that he must identify it, and illegally lifts it and replaces it in such a way that it's sitting up and positively begging to be hit cleanly. We don't want either of these two, even though they remind me of that old gag:

'How can I tell that the ball he is playing with isn't his? Because I've got his in my pocket!'

Then there's the phantom ball marker – you must have met him. He usually has a marker about the size of a 50-pence piece, and this is his ploy. When spotting the ball he places the marker in *front* and not behind. Then when replacing the ball he puts it in front of the marker – gaining possibly two inches.

I remember playing in a four-ball with John Stokes (ex-Bachelors) and a bloke who performed this feat. After a couple of holes, John watched his spotting up ceremony and said:

'Careful now, if you mark that ball once more it'll drop in the hole!'

Mind you, if you think that man is cheating what about the *sliding* ball marker? Have you met him? He has more sleight of hand than Houdini – he could have been a close-up magician, but it probably wouldn't have been as lucrative as playing mugs like us for money.

Picture the ball at rest on the green and up comes this 'magician'. As he begins to place his marker he slides it along the ground, pushing the ball forward with his thumb before placing the marker several inches (and I mean several!) nearer the hole.

No, we wouldn't have him or any of his cronies. Nor would we have the player who can't keep a straight card. You've met him – he always tries to declare a stroke or two less than his actual score, and who's to argue if we haven't kept count? Mister five by five never has a double bogey, and never has a blob in the Stableford.

... always finds his own ball.

On our very special day we want no cheats, no grumblers, no whingers, no bad sports, no miseries. On our day we want honest endeavour, winning ways and lots of fun. Who cares where they come from, we want memorable moments with unforgettable people. We want great deeds to go down in the annals of all-time great stories.

I mentioned the late great Bill Shankly earlier as a hero of mine. Many's the tale that has been put down to the great man. Emlyn ('Crazy Horse') Hughes, ex-England and Liverpool skipper, says that Bill refused to accept any excuse in defeat. No one ever *beat* Liverpool: Liverpool beat themselves.

'I can't understand how we let the game slip,' said Bill.

'We had to play into the wind in the second half,' Emlyn explained.

'Why didn't you play that way in the first half?' asked Bill.

'We lost the toss, boss.'

'What did you call?' asked Bill.

'Heads.'

'Son, I've told you a million times – never call heads!'

I can believe that. I would like to believe another tale which I've heard about Bill but also about one or two other great sportsmen. Bill's tale has it that Liverpool had lost a home game by one goal – the keeper letting the ball run through his legs. Post-match in the changing rooms, Bill glared at the goalie, who eventually said:

'I know boss, I should have kept my legs together.'

'No, son, your *mother* should have kept her legs together!'

Ah, Bill! We'd have you with us on our great day, golfer or no. For where honesty and 100 per cent effort live, so lives your spirit. Under Shankly, Liverpool were winners and I'd like to have more winners with us, if you don't mind. Nigel Mansell, driver supreme, is a golfer of no mean ability, playing off a handicap of three or four. Ian Botham, England's greatest cricket all-rounder, is one of the very few reputed to have put his tee shot on the green at the 10th at The Belfry, so we must have him, too. Bobby Charlton is another supreme sporting ambassador who is also a more than useful golfer. Welcome to my day, Bobby! My word, I'm waxing lyrical now – but why not? It's our special event, isn't it? We can do what we like, invite whom we please.

But amongst all these famous, talented and unforgettable stars, we must leave room for the most important guests of all – the ordinary, everyday club golfers, the hackers, the backbone of our beloved sport. The ladies and gents without whom the game would have no foundation, no tradition, no pride, no honesty and no folklore.

Yes, on the big day they'll all be there in their glory and what is more they'll all play well. No lost balls, no out of bounds, no duffed drives, no miscued chip shots, no bushes, no heather, and above all none of that terrible willow scrub that turns the rough at Birkdale into purgatory. This will be the round they have all dreamed of, the one that makes it all worthwhile. Even if they hit a ball into a bunker, they'll float it out on a cushion of sand just like Gary Player does – and, like him, they'll sink the putt. Boy, we'll have to have a 19th hole as big as Wembley Stadium to house all these good folk but then money would be no object either.

I'm sure you'll agree with my open-ended invitation to the rank and file golfers, even if my celebrity selection misses out a few of your heroes. But there's plenty of room for your own particular favourites, and I'd gladly welcome them all to the fold.

Remember, my musings are only to trigger a few of your own particular thoughts and ideas. If what I write does nothing more than stimulate you to talk about the game and spread the gospel, then it will have achieved its aim. We may come, we may go, but the game goes on. So why does it have this magical gift? What is so special about a sport that all can play and in which millions take delight? Let's spend our final chapter trying to find a few answers.

11

Well Here We Are, But Then Where the Heck Are We?

ISN'T GOLF the living end? Doesn't it sometimes cross your mind to analyse the average day on the course? If we did, I wonder what we'd find? Probably that golf is a game of opposites. Don't you spend hours longing to get to the first tee? Haven't you dreamed of breaking the course record – or at least of beating your previous best score? Don't you wake up sometimes with the quietly confident conviction that this is the day? Come on, lady luck, or whoever is up there, shine down on me just this once. Give me the answer – or, failing that, at least give me a clue!

If you're like me you've had moments when you stand to a ball and just *know* that you're going to knock it out of sight, and you do. The trouble is you can't bottle the moment and repeat it to order. Yes, that really is the trouble isn't it? When we play a bad shot we instinctively know at least a dozen things that we've done wrong. Too near or too far from the ball, take away too quick, head moved, swayed, didn't make a full turn, no follow through, and so on, ad nauseam. Yet when we play a perfect shot, for some reason we can't remember a thing. All we know is that the set-up was good, the take away just right, and so on – and the rest is history. Unfortunately, forgotten history! The trouble with a really good shot is that it is seamless – we are not aware at the time of the various physical actions and sequences that go to make up the stroke. That's what makes it difficult, not only to analyse it bit by bit but to deliberately repeat it.

Have you ever really creamed a shot and felt so little effort was used that if you *really* swung you could knock it twice as far? That's the trap, of course. That's what makes us lurch into the drive, snatching from the top, right shoulder heaving and disrupting the swing plane that gives us good contact and direction and the whiplash action of the shaft that gives us distance.

I bet you've had a run of three or four holes when everything goes exactly to plan and every shot is a winner. Then, just when you're beginning to believe that golf is really an easy old game, the magic leaves you and you couldn't hit an elephant's backside with a banjo? And doesn't that break your heart, aren't you sorry you ever took up this game? Couldn't you just throw the bag of clubs over a cliff? And then, when everything is at its blackest, you hit a peach of a shot that makes the world all right again. Now that's the moment, no two ways about it. That's the exact second, when you hit the one in a thousand, that decides that you'll come back again tomorrow. Forget the bad holes, remember just those special times when it all went right. That's the way you'll play tomorrow – everything just so, no loss of temper, no frayed nerves over a putt, no worries where the drive's going to go. And that's how the circle is complete. You're back to sleep and dreaming of the perfect round.

How long can we keep this up? As long as there's a golf ball and something to hit it with, I suppose. But at least we can ease the burden by remembering some 'dos' and 'don'ts'. No, I'm not going to go all righteous on you. Just let's be practical shall we? Let the realist in us take the reins and lead us to an easier life.

Nobody ever won a major golf classic without help. I mean from the very beginning to the very triumph. Lessons, tips, practice. They are all essentials to the whole game. Confidence never hurt anyone. A putter you're confident in won't hole every putt, but one you don't like won't hole any. Confidence comes from knowing roughly what you can do and doing it and not being too ambitious. So give a little time to practice – use driving ranges if you can't play regularly. Never wait till you're on the course and playing for real before trying something new. You know how seriously brain-damaged you can be after a lesson from the pro, when you're trying to remember all the tips at once.

So spend a little time and effort before the tee shot. Remember that a large percentage of the golfing secrets are in your head. So try to keep the head clear or as clear as the night before allows. Trust your swing. But, mostly, remember that it's only a game.

Bill Shankly used to say: 'If you wake in the morning with your health and strength, then every day's your birthday, son.' Bill was right and we should be grateful we're able to play the world's greatest game – grateful for the good shots we play, and try to learn from them. Never try to take from the game more than we put in. Use golf and enjoy it, don't let it use you.

Most importantly go back to the questions asked in the opening chapter of this book. Why are we playing, what for, what's it all about? Surely we're playing golf to help us relax, to be part of the greatest and most sporting of sports. We are here to improve where we can, to delight in our achievement and that of others – even if it's through gritted teeth!

No matter what calamities befall him in everyday life, the true hacker still needs the pressure and inconvenience of four hours of trudging in wind or rain or sleet or sun (or all of them at once), hacking at a white pellet that seems to have a mind of its own, and a lousy sense of direction. How come the harder we try, the less we achieve? How come a good round of golf can sneak up on you totally by surprise, and, just when you realize how well you're playing, you start dropping shots like confetti?

Another mark of the true hacker is that he is more satisfied with a round of abject failure high-lighted by a well-played 18th hole, than he is with a blistering round marred by three putts on the last? And, if he cannot boast about a well-played round, he takes equal pleasure in boasting about a disastrous one?

What other pastime infuriates its devotees as much as the great game? What other pastime reduces all of its disciples to crass humility? Soccer, cricket, tennis – all are games where the shot is

'Here he comes now, Mother, out of the wind, rain and sleet.
Wet, frozen, smothered in mud – and *still* he'll tell us he's
had a great day!'

played in the heat of the millisecond and then forgotten. None offers the vertiginous sensation of standing over the ball with all day to think about what to do; all day to impress upon yourself the indubitable fact that from a standing start you are going to strike the ball further than in any other game – as long as you don't miss it entirely. And, as you start your backswing, endless details of swing mechanics buzz around in your head. All in all, you'll be lucky to hit the ball off the teeing ground.

Seriously, my friends, who would be mad enough to participate in this crazy ritual? Who would be so seriously maladjusted as to *pay* to be so punished mentally and physically? Who would? We would! Every time, every day if we could, every morning, every afternoon. When we see a pro make a mistake, we don't think pessimistically: 'Well, if he can't do it, why am I bothering?' No, we exclaim, 'Good heavens, you great pudd'n, I could do better than that!'

Golf's all about things like that. Satisfaction in well-played shots, and delight in calamities. Great conversations in well warmed club houses with good company. Winter mornings that begin with a brandy and hand-shake and end the same way. Summer days when the coffee smells extra special and the greens have never been so green or the sunlight so golden.

In the newspaper trade they say there's no such thing as real news – it's just the same old things happening to different people. Golf is the same – the same ritual, the same highs, the same lows, the same hopes, the same disappointments. Except that they are never *quite* the same. And it's that infinite variety of small differences that makes us vow to return tomorrow to more of the same.

So what is golf? For me, at this moment, golf is a two-year-old grandson, already possessing a good swing, staring at the fairways at Swinley Forest and saying to me: 'When I'm big, I'll play here with you. But it's a long way, so you'll have to hold my hand.'

Wrong, Keir! When you're big you'll probably have to hold my shaking hand, and help me with my zimmer frame. But one thing's for certain, son – one day we'll have that game!

PS

The most up-to-date tale to reach yours truly concerns the visitor to a rather snooty club who enquires of the pro:

'What are the chances of eighteen holes today?'

'I'm sorry,' says the pro, 'but you will have to check with the secretary because they're a little picky at this club.'

Secretary is summoned and duly arrives saying:

'We don't just let anybody play here, you know. Tell me something about yourself.'

'Well,' says the visitor. 'I'm a member at Wentworth, Sunningdale...'

'Never mind that,' says the secretary. 'Tell me about yourself and family.'

'Well, I was born into an upper-middle-class family. Attended Eton, went to Oxford and gained an MA Oxon degree first class. Joined the guards and rose to the rank of brigadier. Awarded the vc, DSO and bar in the war. Back in civvy Street I joined the stock market and I'm a director of six companies. Been Lord Mayor of London twice and have been appointed equerry to the Queen.'

'All right,' says the secretary, 'you can go out but just play the front nine where I can keep an eye on you.'

Good put-down story. Good tag.

And on that subject, here's a little homework for you. If you've a golf tale, be it sad, happy, disastrous, miraculous, hilarious, strange, unbelievable or just plain interesting, why don't you write in and tell us about it? Write to Tom O'Connor c/o Robson Books, Bolsover House, 5–6 Clipstone Street, London W1P 7EB and, who knows, you may win one of our star prizes and may even see your story – and your name – in print!